Advance

REMARK

"If you're feeling sucker-punche~~~~~~~~~~~~~~~~~
to ashes and you can muster no hope for the future, hang on to the hope you'll find in these pages. There is a purpose and a plan in the struggle you're facing. And the hope God offers is not only available but ready for the believing. Shauna Letellier has written another dangerous book about people who dared to fully trust in God."

—Chris Fabry, author of *War Room* and
host of Chris Fabry Live

"Shauna Letellier has done a remarkable service for those of us whose hopes in Christ at one time or another have buckled under the weight of some unbearable disappointment. She deftly moves between the first century and our own to give biblical precedent for the legitimacy of our own doubts, questions, and confusion. In doing so, she encourages us by showing that those responses are not distinct from biblical hope but rather are distinctive aspects of it. An affirming devotional for either personal or group use."

—Ken Gire, author of *Moments with the Savior*
and *Windows of the Soul*

"I read *Remarkable Hope* during a season of being blindsided by gut-wrenching disappointment. I'd lost more than hope: I'd lost all sense of direction. Vicariously experiencing Jesus reviving hope in these vividly retold Bible stories helped me regain footing in my own new narrative. In the tender places where your heart is broken, Shauna is a trustworthy guide, gently leading you toward healing, hope, and surprising joy."

—Cheri Gregory, cohost of the Grit 'n' Grace podcast and
coauthor of *Overwhelmed* and *You Don't Have to Try So Hard*

"In *Remarkable Hope*, familiar biblical stories spring to life with new power and perspective, and a newfound hope takes root in the life of the reader. Letellier has done it again!"

—Cindy Lambert, coauthor of *Unplanned*

"Few components of the Christian life are more necessary than hope, but what do we do when hope is shattered? Shauna tackles this question and its variants by guiding us through scriptural accounts of people just like us—full of confusion or consternation, facing a crisis or a crossroad—and how their lives were changed by the One who created, and is bigger than, our hope. Shauna's masterful storytelling drives us into the middle of a stark situation, pulls our heartstrings, and turns a mirror on our feeble attempts to determine what God is up to. This book helps align our expectations with powerful truth and shows us the deeper level of a true and lasting hope."

—Yolanda Smith, writer and editor

"Shauna Letellier is establishing herself as a writer who can not only identify and clarify deep feelings and questions, but also bring biblical meaning and help to people who need it. In *Remarkable Hope*, she again pinpoints specific disappointed people in the Scriptures and gives us a glimpse of what God might be about in their lives. And that is the genius of this book: We see God at work reviving hope in troubled hearts, troubled times.

"Invitingly written, you'll find it hard to put down, and your soul will drink in these life-giving words. Shauna uses biblical characters to show us our own need. She selects theological thinkers to reinforce application for us. This is a blend of substance and emotional connection, perspective and deep passion, help and hope."

—Gregory C. Carlson, PhD, chair and professor of Christian Ministries and Leadership, Trinity International University

REMARKABLE HOPE

WHEN JESUS REVIVED HOPE
IN DISAPPOINTED PEOPLE

SHAUNA LETELLIER

Faith
Words

Nashville   New York

FaithWords / Hachette Book Group
1290 Avenue of the Americas, New York, NY 10104
faithwords.com
twitter.com/faithwords

First Edition: March 2019

FaithWords is a division of Hachette Book Group, Inc. The FaithWords name and logo are trademarks of Hachette Book Group, Inc.

The publisher is not responsible for websites (or their content) that are not owned by the publisher.

The Hachette Speakers Bureau provides a wide range of authors for speaking events. To find out more, go to www.hachettespeakersbureau.com or call (866) 376-6591.

Library of Congress Cataloging-in-Publication Data

Names: Letellier, Shauna, author.
Title: Remarkable hope : when Jesus revived hope in disappointed people /
    Shauna Letellier.
Description: First edition. | Nashville : FaithWords, 2019. | Includes bibliographical
    references.
Identifiers: LCCN 2018037098| ISBN 9781455571710 (trade pbk.) |
    ISBN 9781455571703 (ebook)
Subjects: LCSH: Hope—Biblical teaching. | Bible stories, English—Gospels.
Classification: LCC BS680.H7 L48 2019 | DDC 232.9/5—dc23
LC record available at https://lccn.loc.gov/2018037098

ISBNs: 978-1-4555-7171-0 (paperback), 978-1-4555-7170-3 (ebook)

Printed in the United States of America

LSC-C

10 9 8 7 6 5 4 3 2 1

*For my mother, Cheryl.
You have weathered devastating
disappointments—widowhood, the death
of a son, the puzzle of nurturing a blended
family, grieving for grandbabies you never held,
the hospitalization of children and grandchildren,
ailing parents, and the burdens of your friends
and family. You clung to Jesus. Thank you for
showing me how to live an unexpected life of
remarkable hope in Christ.*

This hope is not an imagination, not the projection of wishes upon the dim curtain of the future, not the child of calculation, but a present reality within arm's length of us all.

—Alexander MacLaren, *Expositions of Holy Scripture*

Contents

Steadfast Hope

Why, my soul, are you downcast?
Why so disturbed within me?
Put your hope in God,
for I will yet praise him,
my Savior and my God.

—Psalm 42:5

Hope. We use the word every day.

I hope it doesn't rain.
I hope you feel better.
I hope I get to sleep in.

With the best intentions, we cast pleasant desires for ourselves and our friends into the air to vanish. We mean well, but we have precious little control over actual outcomes.

> *I hope it doesn't rain. (But there are clouds rolling in.)*
> *I hope you feel better. (But sympathy doesn't chase away the virus.)*
> *I hope I get to sleep in. (But I have young children.)*

Our expressions are also colored with unlikelihood. "Dashed hope" gives way to the announcement that the situation is "beyond hope." Even when we speak positively, hope is a small "glimmer," a singular "ray," or a fine "thread."

Obedience Means Blessing...Doesn't It?

It is a strange and sad irony that our well-wishes are thin and unreliable. In devastation and unmet expectations, we may mistakenly conclude that our hope in Christ is as slippery as the rain we were hoping not to get.

A Christian marriage is destroyed by abuse, addiction, or rebellion. We know parents who "trained up a child in the way he should go"* but found themselves speaking through microphones to their beloved on the other side of bulletproof glass, and we become suspicious of the hope Christ offers.

A series of ongoing calamities can prove just as baffling. For me it was a relocation that was clearly God's direction. It resulted in a nontraveling work schedule that morphed into an eighty-hour workweek. A policy loophole turned a salaried position into an hourly one that didn't include overtime pay. A rented house depleted our savings for a down payment and didn't feel like home. To add insult to injury, I found myself grinding up dog food for eleven yelping puppies in my laundry room while my own newborn preemie lay in an Isolette with a feeding tube in an NICU three hours away.

You could insert your story here too. My string of catastrophes may sound minor if you've endured the miseries of chemotherapy, testified in court against a family member, or purchased a tiny casket.

We have obeyed God and placed our hope in him. We anticipate a life full of blessings tailored to our

---

* Proverbs 22:6

preferences. Instead of feeling blessed, we feel sucker punched.

A Mystery Secured

Hope is a pillar of our Christian faith. It is not the vaporous wish tainted by doubt that we employ as we blow out birthday candles. When the apostles wrote about it, they spoke with confident assurance. Peter tells us we have a "living hope."[*] The writer of Hebrews calls it an "anchor for the soul." Dictionary definitions include, "An expectation of what is sure (certain)."

Biblical hope is expectant certainty. It is knowing that Christ guarantees everything he has promised and purchased.

When Paul prayed for the church in the city of Ephesus he said, "I pray that the eyes of your heart may be enlightened in order that you may know the hope to which he has called you."[†] That kind of hope is no evaporating well-wish. It is absolute—a hope that does not put us to shame.[‡]

---

[*] 1 Peter 1:3
[†] Ephesians 1:18
[‡] See Romans 5:5.

Nothing Less, Nothing More

Hymn writer Edward Mote wrote, "My hope is built on nothing less than Jesus' blood and righteousness." That's true, but it's also built on nothing more. Perhaps that sucker-punched feeling stems from placing our hope in something besides Jesus. Without realizing it, we may have placed our confidence in our spiritual performance to gain the blessings we prefer. Perhaps we've counted on a "promise" that was merely inspirational language. The discovery can disorient us. How can we regain our footing?

Throughout the Gospels we read the accounts of people who hoped in Christ and experienced disappointments ranging from confusion to devastation. Think of the four men who carried their paralyzed friend to Jesus. They laid their silent request before the whole room. Atrophied limbs screamed for help. When Jesus said, "Friend, your sins are forgiven," every observer was either devastated or incensed. They wanted Jesus to restore the body they could see, but Jesus' priority was to revive the soul they couldn't see.*

---

* See Mark 2:1–12.

Surprised by God

When I began scribbling ideas for this book, I could think of a few stories in the Gospels where people felt let down by Jesus. As I studied, I found many more. Pastor and author John Koessler writes, "If the Gospels are any indication, we might even say that disappointment is a certainty. Read the Gospels with all their sharp edges intact. What are they but a record of disappointment with Jesus on a grand scale?"[1]

In each of those sharp-edged stories, Jesus transformed disappointment into unexpected gifts. To look carefully at these Bible stories is to see an ongoing pattern of people being surprised by God's methods in the most drastic ways. His work was rarely what they anticipated but always immeasurably more than they could have asked or imagined.

The following chapters are biblical vignettes: short retellings of times when people placed their hope in Christ and appeared—at first—to be disappointed by him. Eventually, they experienced ultimate freedom instead of physical freedom, a permanent kingdom instead of a political kingdom, a lifelong mission instead of a mission trip.

In each vignette, I have laid the fabric of fiction over the framework of Scripture. Everything God gave in his word is all we need, and storytelling is a powerful tool to help us remember concepts. Jesus used parables often. To teach the value of God's kingdom, Jesus told of a man who bought an entire field because of the treasure buried there. To demonstrate God's response to repentant sinners, Jesus described a father's lavish celebration over the return of his wasteful son. When we unfurl the backdrop of history, humanity, and a few details of sanctified imagination, a concept comes to life.

I have tried to stay close to the Scriptures with these retellings. Where parallel passages were different, I combined the words and accounts of the Gospel writers into one. Where Scripture was unclear on motives, I imagined one I felt was reasonable in the situation. Where Scripture was silent, I sifted through possibilities presented in a variety of Bible commentaries. Then I wove in a little historic, geographic, political, religious, and cultural detail to provide context for the passage.

I operated with the understanding that these Gospel characters had committed much, if not all, of the first five books of our Bible, as well as Psalms, to memory. There are occasions inside these chapters where I have inserted dialogue or prayers. Although they do not appear in the biblical accounts, I assumed the person would be familiar with the Scripture and hymnbook of their day.

My prayer is that through this series of Bible moments retold, we who have clung to Christ will be greatly encouraged. As we observe his faithful commitment to those who hope in him, we will be wowed by his unseen plan, comforted by his words, and revived by his presence. We will finally chime in with Paul and declare that our "hope does not disappoint" us.* Because when we are downcast and disturbed, our hope is in God, who gives more than we can imagine but rarely what we expect.

---

* Romans 5:5 (NASB)

Long-Expected Hope

Simeon Sees the Lord's Messiah

Now there was a man in Jerusalem called Simeon, who was righteous and devout. He was waiting for the consolation of Israel, and the Holy Spirit was on him. It had been revealed to him by the Holy Spirit that he would not die before he had seen the Lord's Messiah. Moved by the Spirit, he went into the temple courts. When the parents brought in the child Jesus to do for him what the custom of the Law required, Simeon took him in his arms and praised God, saying:

"Sovereign Lord, as you have promised,
you may now dismiss your servant in peace.
For my eyes have seen your salvation,
which you have prepared in the sight of all nations:
a light for revelation to the Gentiles,
and the glory of your people Israel."

The child's father and mother marveled at what was said about him. Then Simeon blessed them and said to Mary, his mother: "This child is destined to cause the falling and rising of many in Israel, and to be a sign that will be spoken against, so that the thoughts of many hearts will be revealed. And a sword will pierce your own soul too."

—Luke 2:25–35

In the predawn light of the east-facing window, Simeon knelt on a worn rug folded in half. For a long time, he had never bothered with this luxury, but as the years had passed, it had become a necessity. He settled in and rested his arms in the worn grooves of the low wooden sill. It was polished in two places where his sleeves had buffed the roughness to a shine and worn his tunic thin at the elbows.

Above him sparrows chattered and skittered along the ridge of his roof, occasionally swooping past the window, unstartled by his folded hands hanging over the ledge. Yesterday a brave female had perched on the sill and spied an open bag of wool. She'd fluttered across the room, snatched a bit, and fled. Sparrows were his prayer companions, and he didn't mind sharing a few strands for her nest, but he did tie the bag.

He lifted his face toward heaven. Flaming orange prepared to peek over the Jerusalem skyline, and the sharp angles of the city's buildings were silhouetted against it.

"In the morning, Lord, you hear my voice; in the morning I lay my requests before you and wait expectantly."* A pale brown bird landed beside his sleeve.

"You're awaiting spring?" Simeon asked her. She cocked her head from side to side and eyed his beard, which was ruffled by the breeze. Simeon whispered, "I'm awaiting the Messiah," and she darted back to the roof.

"How long, O Lord?" He'd been asking the same question ever since he'd received the promise. "Will it be today?"

Each day, God had answered with the sunset, *A little longer.* The purple light of the following morning would find him kneeling, expecting God to do what he had promised.

---

* Psalm 5:3

"I will wait for you, O Lord, and you will send your comforter as you have promised. Let the morning bring me word of your unfailing love. I trust in you. Show me the way I should go, for to you I entrust my life."*

Three trumpet blasts startled him from prayer. The daily musical announcement to the devout in Jerusalem floated from the Temple Mount, declaring, "A sacrifice is made for you." Simeon supported himself against the window's ledge, stood, and rolled the rug against the wall.

Sabbath preparations would begin this evening, and he had until sunset to visit his vendors and customers to buy and sell his wool. On this last day of the week, the shearers would be eager to sell so they'd have nothing to carry on the Sabbath. His buyers would be anxious to stock supplies for the following week because tomorrow there would be no trading. Market negotiations would cease. Customers would disappear. Even the weavers' shuttles would rest in the yarn. All attention would be turned toward the temple. It was the law.

The trumpet blasts faded to echoes bouncing off walls. A pot of boiling water sputtered in the fire. Simeon pulled it out and spooned a boiled egg onto

---

* See Psalm 143:8.

the table. He peeled it and popped it in his mouth. The sparrow had alighted on the sill again, and he nodded an apology. "It wasn't yours."

He slung bags of wool over his shoulder and thanked God he was not carrying a pile of dense blankets, as he had when he was younger. He tired easily these days. Clean, combed wool was lighter to carry. Fleece was cheaper for folks to buy than woven goods, and the spinners and weavers would be glad to see him. He would be home long before sunset.

Simeon stepped outside and smelled the morning sacrifice wafting from the temple. A column of smoke billowed heavenward as he walked toward the market. The air was cool, and on the low, west side of the temple a chill clung to the stone streets. Shadows would linger until afternoon, and he was glad for the warmth of the wool resting on his back.

It was a short distance from his house to the temple, and along the street between the two, the market waited for the arrival of its tradesmen and women. Early risers shook open the curtains and swept dust out of their booths. A flock of disoriented lambs clattered through the street as shepherds corralled them into pens. The lambs bleated. *For good reason*, Simeon thought as smoke drifted over the city.

Bakers laid out baskets of barley and loaves as he passed. Money changers sorted currency by region and balanced their scales. Soon the long line of tables would be loaded with rounds of cheese, jars of olive oil, bundles of dried figs, and the last of the almond harvest, long since shaken from their branches. Skins filled with new wine dangled from an awning.

Simeon's interests lay further toward the temple, where the dyers, weavers, and spinners were already at work.

Perched on her stool, Tabitha pulled tufts of wool from her depleted supply. Simeon approached, and she waved him to hurry. Her drop spindle blurred as she twisted it. Wrapping new yarn around the spindle's shaft, she glanced up. "Good morning, Simeon."

He dropped the bags and paused to rub the stiffness from his knuckles before working the knot loose. As she emptied her sack, he opened a new one.

"Thank you, Simeon." Without stopping her work, she dug in a pouch at her waist for her payment. Simeon watched. Pull, twist, dig for coins. Pull, twist, close the pouch. It was the long-practiced dance of fingers that knew no other rhythm. Tabitha shook the coins out of her hand as if they had contaminated her. She leaned toward him and lowered her voice. "As always, I'm sorry to pay with coins bearing a Roman image."

"The Messiah is coming, Tabitha," he reminded her.

"Well, if you find him, don't let the Romans hear of it."

"Peace to you, Tabitha." She nodded, and he hefted the remaining wool onto his back.

Farther on, steam rose from the boiling vats of the dyers and dampened the air. Extracting colors from crushed flowers, Mediterranean snails, and insects created an odor that was pleasing only to those who made a living by it.

A dyer bent over a copper pot, his head obscured by the thick steam. With a rod he jabbed at the wool, forcing it back to the bottom of the pot.

"Peace to you this morning, Benjamin," said Simeon.

Benjamin emerged from the cloud. He dried his hands on his apron, which was spattered with blood and wine, mud and berries.

"Peace to you, Simeon!" Benjamin came to the front to examine the fleece. Decades of staining fabric had left his arms permanently the color of a bruise. He worked his fingers through the fibers and made his usual offer.

By the time Simeon had made his way through the

market, his goods were sold. In addition to coins, he had taken bread and blankets in trade.

The street churned with activity. Beyond the vendors, the needy lined the way to the temple. The blind, crippled, poor, and sick stretched along the street and all along the ramp that ascended to the temple gates. Simeon stepped to the side, rubbed his knuckles again, and dropped coins into the pouch tied inside his cloak.

What was to him a quiet plinking might as well have been a trumpet blast to the nearby beggars— an announcement that help was near. Their pleading drew him. His bread and blankets became heavy.

"Simeon!" one called. They knew him by name and expected his gifts.

"Peace to you." He tore the loaves into chunks and gave them away. It would be chilly again tonight, so he unrolled the blankets as well.

"Have you seen him yet?" asked a blind man.

"Not yet," Simeon answered, draping a blanket over a man with one leg.

"Me neither!" He laughed, and all the beggars joined him.

"I'll tell you when I do," Simeon said as he placed a loaf in his hand.

With mouths full of bread their laughter was garbled. They huddled under the blankets and picked crumbs off the ground.

He understood their skepticism. All of Israel was waiting and hoping for the Messiah to comfort them and deliver them from Roman occupation and to rule them in righteousness forever. In his long life, Simeon had lived through siege and famine, war and drought. In every crisis he had called on the Lord to send the promised one to come near and help.

Decades of shearing and combing had left his hands gnarled and aching. He was tired, but reminders from his aging body heightened his expectancy. Alert as a brittle leaf ready to fly in every breath of wind, Simeon was ready to hail the Messiah any day. It would be soon. It had to be. He would see the Messiah before he died. The Holy Spirit had promised.

Forty years ago, Simeon had heard him.

Hunger and thirst brought on by Herod's five-month siege of Jerusalem had weakened Simeon and the entire city. Assisted by legions of Roman troops, Herod built walls and dug tunnels around the city to force his reign upon them.

Bold and unwilling to surrender, Jerusalem's citizens made their own underground passages to collapse the tunnels and surprise the Romans with their fortitude. As one of the stronger young men, Simeon was commissioned to haul dirt from the countermining efforts. Despite their defensive work, soldiers finally breached the walls. They filed into the city like ants into a hill, sweating and drunk on looted wine, slaying anyone in their way.

The dehydrated Jerusalem soil drank up the blood of its slaughtered citizens.

Hidden underground, Simeon muttered an accusatory prayer. "Now would be a fine time to send the deliverer you promised." Simeon recited God's promises back to him: "You said, if I called upon you, you'd answer. You promised to be with me in trouble and deliver me! For those who love you, you've promised to satisfy them with long life and show them your salvation."*

As if in answer to his recited prayers, an underground breeze tossed together Scriptures scattered in his memory. They tumbled to the fore in what sounded like a gentle whisper.

You will not die until you have seen my Anointed One. He will comfort you. You will see my servant with

---

* See Psalm 91:15–16.

your own eyes in the land of the living. Watch. Wait. Hope. I will do what I have promised.

Days after the siege ended, Simeon crawled from the tunnel. He stepped over bodies in the blood-crusted street and rushed to the temple to fill his lungs with the smoke of burnt offerings rather than the stench of decay. But the outer courts of the temple were smoking remnants of beams chewed by Roman hatchets.

A priest shuffled among the charred pillars, stepping over debris as he carried wood toward the altar. It was the unthinking work of a traumatized man. He could only do what he'd always done. Simeon caught up with him and heard his lament.

"Why do you hide your face, God? Why do you forget our affliction and oppression?"* His cheeks were smeared with soot and tears.

"I remain confident of this," Simeon told the priest, borrowing words from the psalmist. "I will see the goodness of the Lord in the land of the living."† With the heartsick look of a man whose hope had been too long deferred, the priest extended his arm toward the

---

* Psalm 44:24
† Psalm 27:13

gate, inviting Simeon to leave the court and take his youthful expectations with him.

He had left the priest that day and weaved through the burnt remains strewn about this very ramp. Today it was strewn with religious pilgrims.

Jews from Jerusalem and those from far-off cities stepped around the beggars and bustled toward the gate. *Today, Lord?* he asked again. He heard a gentle whisper: *Come and see.*

Simeon startled. Were the beggars mocking him? He turned around. They clamored for coins and food as other worshippers passed. Simeon had meant to return home, but the answer shocked him. He climbed the ramp with the others and filed through the gates into the sprawling open-air courts. Like a beggar, hungry and hopeful, Simeon's heart was on high alert. This was his post—his long-practiced dance. He knew no other rhythm.

Come and see what the Lord has done... * The psalm rose in his mind and heart.

Sunlight reflected at angles off gold flourishes inlaid in the walls and adorning the columns. Money changers lined the outer walls of the court. They exchanged

---

* Psalm 66:5

foreign currency and sold animals for prescribed sacrifices. Lambs cried. Pigeons scratched for grain in their cages and found nothing. Smells of livestock mingled with what remained of the morning incense. Structured and predictable, it was the ordinary rhythm. Over time, worship faded into routine. Praise was diluted to rehearsal, and leadership deteriorated into tyranny.

An elderly woman, bent like a cane, stood under the portico, surrounded by enthralled women. They towered over her tiny frame but leaned in to listen. He waved to her, and she spotted him through the milling crowd. He raised his eyebrows as if to silently ask, *Has he come?* She returned a fragile wave, and he knew Anna, too, was still waiting.

Priests carrying wood and oil from storage greeted Anna as they passed. While the local and foreign worshippers came and went, Anna stayed at the temple. She was a fixture as natural as the portico sheltering her spontaneous prophecies. Anna missed nothing. She heard Scripture read many times a day. She recited prayers long ago memorized through repeated listening. When the Levite chorus performed, she sang along, though Simeon could never hear her. Eight decades of fasting from worldly comfort and feasting on the Scriptures had weakened her body but strengthened her hope. She saw religious corruption and irreverence up close, and yet she remained watchful for the Messiah.

Simeon had been waving to her for years. They visited occasionally, but words weren't always necessary. If she had any indication the Messiah had ridden into Jerusalem or unseated the high priest, she would tell him. She would tell everyone.

The Levite choir assembled on the rounded stairs leading toward the altar and sang. "Better is one day in your courts than a thousand elsewhere."* The lyric came as a welcome invitation to stay.

The ornate floor of the temple courts gleamed, and Simeon shielded his eyes in time to see a young family shouldering through the crowd. The father wrestled a couple of pigeons he'd purchased and wedged them under his arm. His wife consoled the baby, who'd been startled by the commotion. He squealed, and his mother bounced and patted him. A crown of black fuzzy hair nestled below her shoulder. Tiny legs were drawn up to his body. She draped her shawl over him and soothed him.

The dirtied and frayed hems of their cloaks spoke of a long journey. Caring for the baby and corralling

---

* Psalm 84:10

the birds had added to their disheveled appearance. The baby's blanket hung long over his mother's arm and dragged the floor.

They were not the only young parents with a newborn offering their purification sacrifice that morning, but Simeon was captivated by this young family. As they were passing, Simeon said, "Young daughter…" She stopped, and he reached down to hand her the trailing blanket.

"Thank you," said the father. Simeon detected a Galilean accent.

"You've traveled a long way the last few days. Where's home?"

"Home is Nazareth," said the young father.

And he will be called a Nazarene.

"But we've only come from Bethlehem today."

Bethlehem Ephrathah, though you are small among the clans of Judah, out of you will come for me one who will be ruler over Israel.*

Every Scripture he'd wondered about, every circumstance that had given him pause, every prayer he had cried, collided in his mind like drops of oil on water. Simeon blinked into the sunlight, speechless.

---

* Micah 5:2

To ease the awkward silence of his elder, the young father volunteered, "We were there for the census last month."

The baby made little grunting noises as his head bobbed on his mother's shoulder.

"What have you named him?" Simeon asked the father.

"His name is Jesus."

"Is it a family name?"

The young couple hesitated, and finally the mother spoke. "It was the name given to us."

"Jesus," Simeon repeated, and he reveled in the meaning. "God saves."

"That's right," she raised her eyebrows in surprise.

Of course. Simeon nodded. "I had expected someone a little bigger." He smiled, and a tear rolled into his beard.

In that moment, an unspoken kinship of belief knit them together. "I'm Joseph, and this is Mary."

Simeon rubbed the stiffness out of his hands, then reached for the baby. Mary placed her son in his arms. The baby squirmed as he was passed from the warmth of his mother to the rugged arms of a wool merchant.

"God promised I would see him, and now I have." He peered into tiny brown eyes blinking at the brightness.

Placing a wrinkled hand on the baby's head, he lifted his face toward heaven and prayed, "Lord, you can now dismiss your servant in peace. I have seen your salvation, which you have prepared for all people. He is a light to reveal God to the nations, and he is the glory of your people Israel!"*

As Simeon praised God and blessed the parents, his breath moved wisps of hair on the baby's head.

Mary wiped her eyes. Joseph put an arm around her shoulder and pulled her close. "You know, then?" he asked Simeon. "He will save us from our sins."

"Yes," Simeon whispered. "Not only us. Many nations." He nodded with grateful tears.

What comfort. What consolation. They knew who he held. *What willing and surrendered young ones,* he marveled. *God does all things well.* "Son, I have been waiting and watching for this child most of my life. Only, I had been looking for a man. I didn't think to look for a baby."

"God does the unexpected, doesn't he?" Joseph said.

Simeon handed the Savior back to his mother. "And he will continue to."

---

* Luke 2:29–32 (NIV, NLT)

He placed his hands on their shoulders. It grieved him to say it, but he knew he must. The Spirit of God had spoken, and he mustn't keep silent. "This child is destined to cause many in Israel to fall, and many others to rise. He has been sent as a sign from God, but many will oppose him. As a result, the deepest thoughts of many hearts will be revealed."*

He paused. "Not everyone wants to be saved from sin. Not many want their hearts to be revealed." A dull pain worked across his forehead. He let his hand slide to Mary's elbow. Wiping tears into his beard, he gently warned, "I'm afraid a sword will pierce your own soul too, Mary."

Simeon felt a frail hand on his back. Anna had sidled up to him and peered into the mother's blanketed bundle as Simeon nodded and wiped his eyes.

"Thanks be to God!" Her voice, tiny but forceful, cracked. She raised her hands to heaven. "I will thank you, Lord, among all the people; I will sing your praises among the nations."†

She began speaking about the baby as God's promised

---

* Luke 2:34 (NLT)
† Psalm 57:9 (NLT)

Messiah. She recounted God's faithfulness to Israel as a firsthand witness to events her listeners only knew as history. Many had been fooled into following false messiahs. The few in the temple who were also looking for the redemption of Jerusalem listened carefully. They eyed the couple as she cradled the baby and he held the exhausted pigeons.

Simeon's heart pushed hard against his throat. He had been searching at the front of a battalion, behind the curtains of the palace, and at the helm of the temple. But here, among ordinary routine in the temple courts, God had stopped him in time to see. Simeon had waited and hoped to behold the Messiah. He never imagined he would *hold* the Messiah.

A Waiting Watchman

Although Scripture does not mention Simeon's occupation, it does tell us what kind of man he was. Simeon was righteous and devout. We know for sure he was a watchman. Not in the military sense, not perched on the citadels of the Jerusalem walls, but watching from the window of his house, observing from the public courts of the temple, and paying attention to the revolving leadership. He was waiting for deliverance, watching for God's comforter, anticipating the day when God's promise would come to fruition.

Simeon was a man who hoped, but hope deferred makes the heart sick,* and there was much to be sick about as Simeon watched the political and religious landscape of Jerusalem unfold.

So little in Jerusalem pointed to the nearness of the comfort he hoped for. Their king was impulsive and indulgent, their armies weak and always in need of funds and aid from Rome. Their place of worship was corrupted by greed, leadership positions were available for purchase and kept based on one's ability to placate a king and pander to Rome.

Despite a political, religious, and cultural quagmire, Simeon hoped. No one would have blamed him if he hadn't. But Simeon based his hope not on what his eyes could see in his present situation but on God's unbreakable promise and his undeniable past work. He was, as the apostle Paul says, "joyful in hope, patient in affliction, faithful in prayer."†

---

* Proverbs 13:12
† Romans 12:12

The Watchman's Reasons for Hope

Simeon's confident expectation was based on the rock-solid foundation of God's age-old promises. Those who saw them as empty words stumbled over the foundation rather than building on it. What God had declared in the past, he had certainly accomplished. To their father Abraham, God had promised descendants, a land for them to live in, and an eternal blessing from them and for them. Simeon's family was living proof that God had been faithful to his word.

Beyond that, Simeon had the record of Scripture he'd memorized as a boy in the synagogue. Throughout his life, the same record of God's faithfulness to his people—even in their stiff-necked unfaithfulness—was recited at their family Passover meals. On Jewish holidays and for weeks of celebration, they rehearsed entire accounts of God's intervention on their behalf. And every day, in their homes and at the temple, morning and night, they recalled his character: "Hear O Israel: The LORD Your God, the LORD is one."* They were to love the Lord with all their heart, soul, and mind. Memorized

---

* Deuteronomy 6:4

Scripture kept God's words at the front of their minds. Daily worship recalled his work in the sacred places of their hearts. Tassels and engraved doorposts served as physical reminders of his spiritual presence.

But to Simeon, God gave something more. God entrusted Simeon with a personal promise in answer to Simeon's hopeful prayers based on God's word. Beyond the Scripture, beyond God's demonstrated dependability, Simeon also received a specific promise from the Holy Spirit that he would not die until he had seen the Lord's Christ.*

This expectant waiting for what God would certainly do impacted his minutes and his days. Mornings meant possibility. Walks through the market had him studying the men and the leaders. Temple prayer times found him talking with God about what he had and had not seen. Like a watchman expecting a critical messenger, these were the outward responses of a heart on alert for good news, comfort, and peace. Simeon was at his post awaiting the consolation of Israel. It was just a matter of time.

And when the set time had fully come, God sent his Son.†

---

* Luke 2:26
† See Galatians 4:4.

A Promise That Can't Be Missed

That day in the temple, God ordained a meeting of his righteous and regular servants. Mary and Joseph were obediently doing what the law required. Scripture was embedded in Simeon's memory, and worship at the temple was embedded in his schedule. When he came to the temple that day, he was doing what he'd always done. Waiting. Watching.

King David describes this kind of watchful hope in a song: "I wait for the Lord, my whole being waits, and in his word I put my hope. I wait for the Lord more than watchmen wait for the morning, more than watchmen wait for the morning."*

Although Simeon expected the Messiah to be a grown man, God in his faithfulness would not allow him to miss seeing the Messiah in his infancy. The promise, its fulfillment, and Simeon's recognition were in God's hands all along.

God can use, and has used, dramatic means to communicate with and lead his people. Being led by the Holy Spirit can mean flashes of light, thunder that

---

* Psalm 130:5–6

sounds like words, or an audible voice. But he is also sovereign over your routines and your trifling decision to leave early or stay late. He can use the plain ingredients of seemingly inconsequential Bible reading or unmemorable sermons to speak in a still small voice on a Tuesday as you're brushing your teeth. He is sovereign over your seeing. He will ensure you recognize the Light of the World even if you're looking for lightning.

Comforting the Comforter

When certain future hope became undeniable present reality, God surprised Simeon with two delights. First, the Comforter arrived as a baby in need of comfort. And second, Simeon himself not only saw the Lord's Christ but held him in his arms.

Deferred hope makes the heart sick, but a longing fulfilled is a tree of life, and the fruit it bore in Simeon's heart came out as a song.* While Simeon welcomed this reality, there was an element of expectation and hope that continued. In the following years, while the baby became a man, all who were waiting

---

* Proverbs 13:12

for the redemption of Israel continued to expect Jesus to deliver them. But the deliverance would not come from the shedding of Roman blood. He did not offer a lamb as a payment for their sins. His deliverance would surprise, disappoint, and offend. Jesus was the lamb, and his blood was shed to save them.

What a beautiful mingling of certainty and surprise, of fulfillment and an unexpected twist. It is the promise of God we count on and expect, but it is his divine right and pleasure to surprise us even while doing exactly what he said. It's why the apostle Paul praised God by saying: "Now to him who is able to do immeasurably more than all we ask or imagine, according to his power that is at work within us, to him be glory in the church and in Christ Jesus throughout all generations, for ever and ever! Amen."*

Modern-Day Watchers

We are millennia away from Simeon's culture, and yet the similarities shock and encourage. We too are waiting, not for Christ's first coming but for his second

---

* Ephesians 3:20–22

coming. We are waiting for answers to decades of prayer. We are counting on God's promises given to us in Scripture. It seems he is long in coming. His answers appear to be delayed. First-century questions still lurk within our hearts: "Where is this 'coming' he promised? Ever since our ancestors died, everything goes on as it has since the beginning of creation."* But questions cannot extinguish the hope secured for us by God's character, work, and reliability.

The apostle Paul reminds us that "whatever was written in earlier times was written for our instruction, so that through endurance and the encouragement of the Scriptures we might have hope *and* overflow with confidence in His promises."† We have the treasure of Scripture set on tables, stacked on shelves, and tucked in pockets. We have the recorded history of Christ's life, death, and resurrection, and we have the New Testament to explain it.

Because God has revealed himself in Scripture we can learn, persevere, and be encouraged. The result is that we have hope—a confident expectation.

---

* 2 Peter 3:4
† Romans 15:4 AMP

In keeping with his character—which loves to startle, surprise, and delight his children—we can hope with certainty that his presence in our lives and his promised eternal kingdom will be immeasurably more than all we could ask or imagine, even if it's not exactly what we expect.

~

Dear Lord,

Thank you for providing the immovable foundation of your spoken and written word. Because of your glory and goodness, you have given me very great and precious promises!*

I confess I have a habit of tweaking them to my liking. I prefer to contort them into promises I understand and visualize.

Help me remember you are not confined by what I can conceive.

---

* 2 Peter 1:3–4

When you display your faithfulness in strange and fantastic ways, point me to the truth that you have spoken and accomplished plans I could never have imagined. Magnify your glory and draw me to you.

Thank you for the delightful assignment of showing the world how to hope in you.

Questioning Hope

John the Baptist in Prison

John's disciples told him about all these things.
Calling two of them, he sent them to the Lord to
ask, "Are you the one who is to come, or should we
expect someone else?"

When the men came to Jesus, they said, "John
the Baptist sent us to you to ask, 'Are you the one
who is to come, or should we expect someone
else?'"

At that very time Jesus cured many who had
diseases, sicknesses and evil spirits, and gave sight
to many who were blind. So he replied to the
messengers, "Go back and report to John what you
have seen and heard: The blind receive sight, the
lame walk, those who have leprosy are cleansed, the
deaf hear, the dead are raised, and the good news is

proclaimed to the poor. Blessed is anyone who does
not stumble on account of me."

—Luke 7:18–23
Parallel Passage: Matthew 11:1–15

A grinding screech shook John from sleep, and
voices bounced off the walls. A beam of light grew
wider and lit up the prison. He gathered his wits to
make an assessment while there was light. His wrists
were scarred and calloused under the iron shackles.
Wounds had scabbed and reopened over the months.
He scrambled to stand and strained against the
chains to see who had let in the light.

Splashing in the corridor made prisoners groan and
revel. The guard who brought water stepped into each
cell, refilling each prisoner's clay water pot. Stepping
toward John he righted the water pot with his foot and
filled it. John lifted it and gulped frantically while it was
fresh. It dripped from his chin and dampened his tunic.

"Easy, Baptist," he said. "I may not be back for a
while."

John gasped for a breath. "Why?" He wiped his hands
on his camel-skin tunic, and examined them for cuts.

"Herod's throwing one of his parties. We've been

carrying water from the spring up to his palace all week. Warm baths and the cold pool are full now, but the palace cistern isn't."

John shivered at the thought of a bath and an over-flowing cistern. The waters of Jordan, flowing gentle and cool, beckoned, and he longed to return to the ministry that had been ripped from him.

The man chained beside John interrupted. "Water..." he whispered. The guard kicked the prisoner's pot toward him and filled it. He laid limp, then lifted one weak finger toward his water. His cracked lips mouthed the word again. *Water.*

He was too weak, and John knew it. John pulled at his own chains until they were taut. Barely able to reach the man, John poured a trickling drink over the man's mouth. He lapped and slurped but didn't open his eyes.

"Won't be long for him," said the guard.

"Bring him bread then," demanded John.

"I'll drown myself in Herod's pool before I tell him to feed his prisoners! Herod doesn't like being told what to do." He laughed. "But I thought you knew that."

"He would do well to listen to either of us," John said as the guard moved down the corridor. He spilled and sloshed, and John grieved the wasted water being swallowed by the floor.

John could not see the door or the entry. But the light streaming in made his head ache. Pressing his fingers over his eyes, he rubbed out the pain.

The guard passed in front of John on his way out. "Tell your visitors to bring him bread," he said as he stomped up the stairs.

The door screamed shut. Darkness relieved his eyes. He backed up to the stone wall to which he was chained and slid to the floor. The floor was damp and sticky. John shivered.

"Water…" the man beside him whispered. But John couldn't see.

"When it's light," he promised.

"Water…"

"I will tell you about water." There was no response, but John continued. "The prophet Isaiah says that the Messiah will open the eyes of the blind and unstop the ears of the deaf. Then will the lame leap like a deer, and the mute tongue shout for joy. Water will gush forth in the wilderness and streams in the desert. The burning sand will become a pool, the thirsty ground bubbling springs."*

The only response was a wheeze.

---

* Isaiah 35:5–7

"I used to speak to many on the banks of the Jordan River. Now I speak to you." John waited, listening for breath. "The kingdom of heaven is near. The wrath of God is coming! You must turn from your sin. Jesus Christ is the Messiah we've been waiting for. I was appointed to prepare the way for him."

"You say he's coming down here?" taunted another prisoner whom John could not see. "You've prepared the way for him to descend to Herod's prison, have you?"

John answered with the words of Isaiah: " 'God has sent me to bind up the brokenhearted, to proclaim freedom for the captives and release from darkness for the prisoners, to proclaim the year of the Lord's favor and the day of vengeance of our God.' "*

"It appears God's vengeance has already come for you," the prisoner mocked as he rattled his chains.

"Water..." The weak refrain came again, and John felt for his water jar to see if he could manage the task in the darkness.

John spoke to him of their plight in the lyrics of a song. " 'We are the ones who sit in darkness. We are the prisoners suffering in iron chains.' " John tried to sing the psalm as he had learned, but he was weak,

---

* Isaiah 61:1–2

and he whispered instead. "'Then they cried to the Lord in their trouble, and he saved them from their distress. He brought them out of darkness, the utter darkness, and broke away their chains.'"*

John stopped, listening for any response. There was none. "'Let them give thanks to the Lord for his unfailing love and his wonderful deeds for mankind, for he breaks down gates of bronze and cuts through bars of iron.'"† His throat tightened and his eyes burned. Drawing his knees to his chest, he muffled a sob in his elbow. His body demanded rest. With visions of God's glory burning through the prison door, melting the shackles off his wrist, John fell asleep and dreamt.

~

He steadied himself in the current. Water rippled past carrying reeds and twigs to the Dead Sea. He dug his feet firmly in Jordan's muddy bed. Thousands had walked from Jerusalem to see the spectacle, and John

---

* Psalm 107:10, 13–14
† Psalm 107:15–16

marveled. They spread along the shore in the groups they'd traveled with.

Directly before him a group of five men from three generations pointed toward him in the water as if to say, "There he is!" The young men dropped their bed rolls. The day's journey from Jerusalem had wearied the grandfather. He leaned against a tree and drank from the skin of water he carried.

Farther down, a group of religious leaders gathered. They eyed the throng and conferred together. Soldiers stationed themselves among the crowd and pretended to keep order, all the while distracted by the peculiar prophet and his forceful message.

John shouted, "Turn away from your sin, and turn toward God! Believe his good news because the kingdom of God is near!" A woman came running from the bank, splashing toward him through the shallows. She confessed her litany of secret sins and broken promises. Her tearful story was her own, but John's response was always the same. He plunged her into the current and drew her out again. *Oh God, I was made for this,* John prayed as he helped her back to dry ground.

One after another they waded in, rambling confessions in sorrow and fear. But not everyone was thrilled with the gathering. Religious leaders who'd come from Jerusalem to see the irritating spectacle had to extract temple taxes from these worshippers. But for John the Baptist, the same devout pilgrims willingly ventured into the desert. They gladly slept outdoors, ate what they brought, and listened to a wild-eyed prophet. While the temple was the center of worship for their nation, John had what the religious rulers did not: Authority. Boldness. Certainty.

They were curious and fearful. It wouldn't be long before his message of a new kingdom and the coming Messiah reached the high priest and then King Herod. John's proclamation of a new kingdom was not welcome news for the current king. He brushed long wet hair from his eyes and scanned the shore for the Messiah.

The sun sank behind the mountains and a desert chill made him shiver. He waded onto the bank. His camel-skin garment was soaked and heavy, and water tapped the ground as it dripped. He bent to wring out the edge, and a trickle ran through his fingers into the river.

John shivered and woke. The water through his fingers was not the brisk river but a chilly puddle. He had knocked over the water pot and it rolled at his side.

Wiping his hand on his cloak, he tilted his head to the ceiling and covered his face.

He cried as he whispered a prayer: *I delighted to do your will, God. I cried in the desert, and by your mercy many hearts were turned toward you! I preached to the people, the leaders, and our wicked king. But you have cut off the work you assigned to me. Isaiah wrote that the Messiah would bind up the brokenhearted and proclaim freedom for the captives and release from darkness for the prisoners. And yet...*

The links of his chains clinked together as he dropped his hands from his face.

In his mind he recalled the fluttering of the Spirit settling on Jesus as John had pulled him up out of the water. The current had rushed softly, and a voice like thunder had declared, "This is my Son."

*Lord, do not forsake me; do not be far from me, my God.**

The prison door burst open and the corridor exploded with sunlight. John pressed filthy hands over his eyes to ease the pain. Boots clattered on the stairs. "Baptist!"

---

* Psalm 38:21

"I'm here." A torch flickered and bounced as two silhouettes shuffled down the corridor toward him. The light was blinding. As much as he ached to see, he closed his eyes again.

"John?"

He turned his head, squinting. The salve of familiarity washed over John, and his voice cracked. "Andrew?"

"Yes, and Philip is with me. I have water." John opened his eyes and saw a jar being lifted to his mouth. He drank, coughed, then drank some more. His beard dripped, and he caught the drops in his hands so they wouldn't be wasted.

Andrew handed him a chunk of bread, and John began devouring it. "Where is Jesus? Has he come with you?"

Andrew hesitated. "He's in Galilee."

John stopped chewing. "He's not baptizing at the river?" he mumbled with his mouth full. He had wanted his own ministry to decrease and that of Jesus to grow, but he'd never imagined Jesus might abandon the work. "Is he baptizing in Galilee?"

"No . . . but he's doing more."

"Baptizing with fire? Has he unseated Herod? Is he ruling at the temple?" John fired possibilities like arrows from a quiver.

"No," Philip answered. "But the crowds who followed you are now following him. He teaches them, John. He doesn't teach like the temple leaders. He teaches with authority, and they hang on his words."

"Are the Pharisees listening?"

"They are listening, but not learning," said Andrew. He leaned forward and lowered his voice. "Actually, they hate him because the tax collectors and prostitutes are coming to him." He paused to gauge John's reaction. "He shares meals with them, and they turn away from their sin."

Philip interrupted. "But he's also amassed a large following because of the signs and miracles he does." Philip scooted toward John. "He heals lepers, and he healed Peter's mother-in-law—did you meet her?" He didn't stop long enough for John to answer. "And a few days ago, we were about to enter Nain when a funeral procession came out of the city gate. The dead man's mother was wailing, and Jesus went right up to the dead man being carried out and he said, 'Young man, get up!' And, John"—Phillip paused, and John held his breath—"that dead man sat up. Jesus gives dead people life!"

Philip came up for air. John glanced at his dying cellmate and lifted his chained wrists. "Herod still rules and keeps me here because I have spoken God's truth to him. Annas and Caiaphas still corrupt the temple, and Israel is still the slave of Rome."

Their conversation had chased the mice away, but the light of the torch emboldened the rodents to return. They skittered and chewed at his cellmate's filthy cloak.

"Will you do something for me?" John turned to Philip and Andrew. "Go ask Jesus, 'Are you the Messiah we've been expecting, or should we keep looking for someone else?'"

He saw their shock that after everything they'd reported, he would still ask. He had been certain before—certain and hopeful that God's plan would be rolled out in Jerusalem and beyond. From the river, with water running off his elbow, he had pointed to the shore and shouted that Jesus was indeed the Messiah. He had warned leaders of God's judgment, which was sure to be quick and soon.

But that was before he'd been summoned to the palace to entertain Herod. Before he'd rebuked him for his incestuous adultery. Before he'd become the object of Herod's wife's wicked schemes. Before his unjust imprisonment. Before his hope had suffocated in this thick and fetid darkness.

"Of course, John. We'll come back with his answer."

John nodded. He knew they would. Jesus would answer.

"You come back, and you better have bread for all of us!" The angry demand came from down the corridor. Andrew and Philip rose to leave.

"Tend to him first," John said, nodding toward the dying prisoner beside him. His lips were cracked and bleeding. They dripped water into his mouth and dropped breadcrumbs on his tongue. Somehow, he swallowed.

———

Days lingered. Weeks wore on. Locusts clicked and buzzed as if taunting him from outside the prison. He grabbed at the dark, dreaming they were within reach but captured only air. Something small skittered away. He swatted in its direction until the chain reined in his frenzied batting. He panted. His heart beat with the wildness of a person thrust from sleep into an icy river. Whether it was morning or evening he couldn't tell. Two things were certain. He was no longer dreaming, and the prisoner beside him was dead. The stench invited vermin.

From far above him and outside the prison, John heard the lilt of music. He opened his eyes, but there was only darkness. The lively plucking of strings soothed his mind. Men whistled and applauded. The aroma of roasting meat seeped into the prison, and John inhaled as if it would fill him up.

Andrew and Philip had returned with Jesus' answer. Jesus was doing much of what they expected the Messiah to do, but not everything. At least not yet. They brought instruction from Jesus to John, saying, "He said you'll be blessed if you don't take offense at him or fall away on account of him." They had also delivered food. But they had not declared freedom, nor a promise of restored ministry, nor any news of Jesus' need for him to continue to prepare the way.

John pulled the last chunk of bread from inside his garment, where he'd put it to keep it from the mice.

Suddenly the door burst open, and the dim light told John it was evening. The raucous cheers of drunken men tumbled down the stairs, and guards argued at the door.

"Tonight?"

"Yes! Hurry up, or it'll be your head on a platter."

"The king insisted we keep him here!"

"Well, Herod is intoxicated and proud of himself. Do you want to argue with him in front of his guests?"

Two soldiers rounded the corner and marched down the corridor, their boots clattering in unison. They stopped in front of John. One held a torch, the other a sword.

"You the Baptist?" one asked.

"Yes."

They swooped in, and in an instant one soldier's boot was on his neck. John's face was on the prison floor, his teeth grating against the stone.

The sword hissed as it was unsheathed. Light exploded in the brightest corridor he'd ever seen, but it did not hurt his eyes.

A voice like rushing water echoed in the radiance, "Well done!"

No One Greater than John

If anyone understood the confusion of deferred hope, it was John the Baptist. From prison, John questioned Jesus, and Jesus still commended him: "Among those born of women there has not risen anyone greater than John the Baptist."*

John himself was the subject of Old Testament prophecies. His mission was prophesied four hundred years prior to his birth. His conception was foretold by the angel Gabriel. Filled with the Holy Spirit from birth, he spent his childhood learning from his aged parents that his cousin, Jesus, was the Messiah generations of Hebrews had hoped for. In adulthood, John kept his vows to God and lived in the desert. With his untrimmed hair tangled by the elements of the Judean wilderness, John was clothed in the yellow fur of a camel. He scavenged honey from buzzing hives and pounced on swarms of locusts to feed himself.

Like those of the prophets before him, his life was a spectacle that drew attention to God's message. But unlike previous prophets, John had the benefit of seeing with his eyes what other prophets had only seen by faith.

In his late twenties, God spoke to him in the desert. His preparation was complete. God directly communicated when his ministry would start, what to do, and who to look for. In obedience, John baptized

---

* Matthew 11:11

Jesus, submerging him and flexing to raise him back up, only to discover something he recognized as the Spirit of God settling on Jesus like a dove. A voice declared, "This is my Son, whom I love; with him I am well pleased."*

A lifetime of direct communication from God produced boldness. From the shore to the temple and in the palace of a bloodthirsty king, John preached, "Repent!"

Descending into Greatness

The first-century historian Josephus wrote that John the Baptist held such great sway over the people that "they seemed ready to do anything he should advise."[2] From the height of his obedience, John foretold the rest of his story without understanding the extent of it: "He must become greater; I must become less."† From that time forward, Jesus' disciples began baptizing more people than John had. John was taken out of circulation when Herod ordered him arrested,

* Matthew 3:17
† John 3:30

bound, and unjustly imprisoned. Old Covenant prophet and New Covenant King crossed paths, and the ministry effectively changed hands.

Disappointment and Doubt

After John was imprisoned, Jesus didn't hurry to the prison to rescue or console him. Although John had visitors and communication with the outside world, as far as we know, Jesus didn't visit him. Instead, he traveled north into Galilee, some seventy miles away. In John's estimation, and in the eyes of those who knew his plight, John had indeed "become less." In a dark prison adjacent to Herod's opulent summer palace at Machaerus,[3] John's certainty withered.

Surely John longed to see God's glory manifested in the Messiah, but it doesn't appear that John witnessed many miracles. He'd been preaching about the coming kingdom, but a visit to the palace landed him in prison. John hoped for freedom from prison and protection from a queen who wanted him dead.

We don't blame him for questioning. When John sent the disciples to ask Jesus if he was the Messiah, Jesus didn't scold him. He didn't explain himself or reason with John about his methods. What Jesus gave was a divine pat on the back and a bit of encouragement. "John, you've done well. I am exactly who you think I am, but my ways are unexpected, and my means are surprising. Trust me, and you'll be blessed."

Home Free

With a lifetime of preparation, a year of ministry, and a couple years in prison, John had served the purposes of God for his life within a short thirty years. The deliverance was swift and permanent. To be absent from the body is to be present with the Lord,* and as John's spirit stepped through the thin divider between earth and heaven, his faith became sight. In that moment, John saw the unveiled glory of God and recognized his voice. "Well done, good and faithful servant!"†

Blessing, deliverance, freedom, and glory were not chance possibilities for John. His hope in Christ gave him certainty that they had already been secured for

---

* See 2 Corinthians 5:8.
† Matthew 25:23

him. But when God brought them about, they were immeasurably more than he'd imagined.

Strength for Today, Bright Hope for Tomorrow

Deprivation wreaks havoc on mind, body, and soul. But it doesn't take a prison cell to wither one's assurance. All it takes is a misguided expectation that goes unmet, and we doubt God's goodness, sovereignty, and love. We find ourselves asking with John, "Jesus, are you who you claim to be? Because you didn't do what I thought you should." Inadvertently we have followed John's example of taking our questions to Jesus. Our persistent questions show we believe he can answer, even if there is a drawn-out silence before his answer comes.

How does Jesus respond to honest and disappointed questions? He says, "Trust me, and you'll be blessed."

What if the waiting is horrible and hard? What if his blessing is unimaginable? What if his deliverance is absolute? What if the reality of God's glory is immeasurably more than its earthly manifestation?

We will trust him to provide the reward he's already secured—that future certainty that doesn't perish, spoil, or fade. "This inheritance is kept in heaven for you, who through faith are shielded by God's power until the coming of the salvation that is ready to be revealed in the last time. In all this you greatly rejoice, though now for a little while you may have had to suffer grief in all kinds of trials. These have come so that the proven genuineness of your faith—of greater worth than gold, which perishes even though refined by fire—may result in praise, glory and honor when Jesus Christ is revealed."*

Our hopes and expectations in this world are shadows compared to the mysterious but secured hope prepared for those who trust Jesus.

Death is not defeat. It is deliverance into all God has prepared for those who love him.

Dear Lord,

Unmitigated suffering is hard to swallow. I hear the news. I have friends and family who suffer injustice. Imprisoned by a list of things I thought

---

* 1 Peter 1:4–7

you would do, I start to wonder, "Are you really in control?"

I confess I've doubted your goodness. You don't always do what I think you ought.

Help me trust that you are working on a grander plan with implications and consequences in an unseen realm. Through your word and your Spirit, fortify my hope. May it not wither in the darkness of doubt. If it does, Lord, gently use my angry questions to lead me back to you.

Help me see that your presence has no boundaries. You are with me in the pleasant light of fruitful ministry and in the devastating darkness of suffering.

Sustain me, Lord, I pray.

Redirected Hope

A Demon-Possessed Man

They went across the lake to the region of the Gerasenes. When Jesus got out of the boat, a man with an impure spirit came from the tombs to meet him. This man lived in the tombs, and no one could bind him anymore, not even with a chain. For he had often been chained hand and foot, but he tore the chains apart and broke the irons on his feet. No one was strong enough to subdue him. Night and day among the tombs and in the hills he would cry out and cut himself with stones.

When he saw Jesus from a distance, he ran and fell on his knees in front of him. He shouted at the top of his voice, "What do you want with me, Jesus, Son of the Most High God? In God's name don't torture me!" For Jesus had said to him, "Come out of this man, you impure spirit!"

Then Jesus asked him, "What is your name?"

"My name is Legion," he replied, "for we are many." And he begged Jesus again and again not to send them out of the area.

A large herd of pigs was feeding on the nearby hillside. The demons begged Jesus, "Send us among the pigs; allow us to go into them." He gave them permission, and the impure spirits came out and went into the pigs. The herd, about two thousand in number, rushed down the steep bank into the lake and were drowned.

Those tending the pigs ran off and reported this in the town and countryside, and the people went out to see what had happened. When they came to Jesus, they saw the man who had been possessed by the legion of demons, sitting there, dressed and in his right mind; and they were afraid. Those who had seen it told the people what had happened to the demon-possessed man—and told about the pigs as well. Then the people began to plead with Jesus to leave their region.

As Jesus was getting into the boat, the man who had been demon-possessed begged to go with him. Jesus did not let him, but said, "Go home to your own people and tell them how much the Lord has

done for you, and how he has had mercy on you."
So the man went away and began to tell in the
Decapolis how much Jesus had done for him. And
all the people were amazed.

—Mark 5:1–20

Parallel Passages: Matthew 8:28–34, Luke 8:26–39

Thunder rolled southward, and the sea below was
calm again. High above the water, inside a limestone
cave, an animal of a man paced and panted. Rainwater
dripped from his naked body, and he shivered. Around
his ankle an iron cuff tore his skin, and links of a broken chain trailed him as he limped. They clinked
against the floor, jangling an indictment with every
step. *Bind him*. Step. *Guard him*. Step. *Kill him*. Step.

The racket grated on him. The cuff had to come
off. He ran out of the cave, the dwindling storm barely
spitting on him now. In the dark he tripped on a rock
and tumbled down the face of the hillside. Chain links
lashed at his legs as he rolled. Crawling back to the rock,
he dug it out of the mud and carried it to the cave.

He crouched and twisted his shackled ankle to the
side. Hoisting the rock above his head, he aimed for
the iron and slammed the weight down. It slipped and

peeled flesh from his foot. He howled and rolled, relishing and reviling the pain. On impact, a shard had clattered on the floor like a dropped knife. Grabbing the makeshift weapon, he limped into the night. With shaking hands, he stabbed his leg and screamed in pain and thrill. Blood dripped toward his feet as he ran, leaving the hillside dotted with bloody footprints.

Running warmed him, but he tired and ducked inside another cave. It was occupied. Another man bellowed at him to leave, and he whipped the shard at him in retaliation and fled.

He ricocheted down the slope full of cavernous tombs. Some were closed by heaps of rubble. He'd opened others, dismantling the piles and hurling stones toward the sea. On the rare occasion when travelers could be seen on the road below, it was an intoxicating thrill to aim at them.

Deafening voices no one else heard drove him. *Run!* He obeyed. He climbed the ridge and heard the soft grunting of sleeping pigs. The air was thick with dampened dung. Each step splashed mud into his self-inflicted wound. Blood pulsed. Warm, sticky, and textured with the grit of his roaming, it dripped and congealed. He crawled into an open tomb ripe with decay, knowing the corpse would not protest.

Below him, the last of the runoff drained toward the water's edge, where the lake swallowed it. On the placid surface, the moon's long reflection shimmered toward the shore, where a hull scraped onto the beach and broke the maddening silence.

He froze, motionless as the corpse inside the cave where he had collapsed. Two fishing boats wobbled and creaked as their passengers stepped ashore. He held his breath. Silhouettes, tired and slow, ambled against the backdrop of the silver lake. Local residents knew better than to pass this way, especially at night. The voices had made sure of it. *Ignorant strangers.*

Then it seized him. He roared toward the shore and flung himself out of the tomb. Arms flailing, legs churning, he flew toward the disembarking men. Rolling gravel chased him down the bank.

Fishermen shouted to one another, "Get back in! Let's go!" Scurrying to untie the ropes they had just secured, they hustled to pull everyone aboard.

Driven by demons, he salivated as they scrambled for ropes and knives. He wanted a fight. But without warning, the demon inside thrust him to the sand and pressed his head toward a stranger's sandals.

The stranger did not recoil.

Demons held him fast. His shoulders cramped,

and his neck twisted hard to one side. He growled, threading his fingers together and twirling them round. For a long time he had roamed, ruling this domain with brutality as an untamable servant of devils. But now he could not raise his head.

"Come out of him, you evil spirit!" said the voice above him.

Shoulders shaking, he stayed, knees planted in the sand. He heard himself say, "What do you want with me, Jesus, Son of the Most High God?" Before the answer came, he pounded the ground and pleaded, "Swear to God that you won't torture me!"

"What is your name?" Jesus demanded.

Name? He'd had a name once. But before he could remember or pronounce it, the evil spirit inside answered for him.

"My name is Legion," he replied, "for we are many." His hair hung long and matted, like moss draped from the canopy of a tree. He tugged and scratched as it dripped around his face. Wringing his hands, he screeched, "Don't order us into the Abyss!"

His voice dropped, and a guttural plea erupted. "Don't send us away!" Voices begged for mercy, and his body bent in fear.

Sunshine spilled over the horizon and painted the

lake orange. A drove of pigs grunted and rooted on the bluff above them. Swineherds called to one another from among their herd.

In the buzzing tone of a whip cutting the air, another voice cried, "If you drive us out, send us into those pigs."

To the legion of spirits spewing out pleas, Jesus shouted, "Go!"

~

The man slumped in the sand. Had he fallen asleep? When had he last slept? He opened his eyes to see a broken iron cuff sinking in the sand beside him. Ripples lapped at the seaside boulders. He sensed men standing above him who didn't dare breathe. Someone had draped a tunic over him and threaded his arms through the sleeves.

High on the bluff above him, a pig squealed, startling them all. Swineherds shouted until they were drowned out by the shrill herd. The low thundering of a legion of hooves rattled gravel from the face of the cliff. Like a waterfall, swine poured over the ridge and churned the water below. Bodies thumped.

Bones snapped. Pigs choked. He covered his ears, curled toward his knees, and rocked.

He knew what it was. That legion had ruled him with an appetite for death. He gasped for air. *It would have been me.*

The men in the boats and on the beach stood stunned, staring into the foaming sea. The entire herd floated and twitched. Stupefied men on the bluff raced toward town and disappeared over the ridge.

Jesus knelt beside the man as he sat up. His body felt limp—not weak, but as if years of constant strain had rushed out of his limbs with the spirits.

One of the fishermen handed Jesus a skin of wine from the boat and he flushed the wound on the man's leg. The man winced. The sight of his own blood no longer thrilled him.

"Where do you stay?" Jesus asked.

He pointed to the hillside pocked with open tombs and decaying bodies, a home for the homeless among the dead. His outstretched hand revealed rope burns encircling his wrists. A web of scars and scabs wrapped his arms. On his leg, the self-inflicted gash throbbed as the wine did its cleansing work. His ankle bled where the iron manacle had chafed.

Every sensation he'd lacked for so long returned in

a rush. Scents of moss and soggy reeds lingered in the humid air. Sunshine warmed his back.

Wonder replaced anger, and his chest ached. It worked its way into his throat, and as Jesus cleaned the wound, a droplet tickled his face. He brushed it away and rubbed the sting from his eyes. He couldn't remember the last time he'd cried. Could he be different, with one word from this Son of God?

"You drove the spirits out of me into those pigs," he said.

"Yes, I did."

Farther up the beach, one of the men who had come with Jesus crouched on a limestone slab. He blew into kindling and waved his hand through a thread of smoke. Another man sloshed through the shallows toward the fire, dragging a net quivering with fish.

"James!" Jesus shouted, "Bring the bread."

They gathered around the fire for a feast of roasted fish, barley loaves, and water—a meal he didn't have to scavenge or steal. They ate, and he marveled. Jesus had stepped ashore, and moments later he could rest, think, and eat. "Where have you come from?" he finally asked.

"We came from Galilee yesterday," James answered, brushing crumbs from his beard.

The fire crackled and a fillet sizzled in its skin. Jesus stirred coals with a stick and the rising heat wrinkled the air as the man stared at him. "You really are the Son of God."

"I am," Jesus answered.

Around the fire, the men stared into the flames.

On the bluff the swineherds reappeared. "He's still there!" Townspeople joined them. In a matter of minutes, a mob bent on vengeance cascaded over the ridge and descended upon the beach. There was nowhere to hide from them. He'd never hidden from them before. He'd always been hungry for their scorn. They shouted accusations and circled him. One jabbed a staff into his ribs. "What have you done now?"

He stood to explain, to tell what Jesus had done, but they scampered backward and threatened. A blacksmith covered in soot jangled a chain and shouted, "Get back!"

He ducked as the chain zipped past his head. "I'm not who I was!" he pleaded with them. "This Jesus is the Son of God. He has rescued me!" He wrapped his arms over his head for protection and braced for another blow.

"Son of God? He's still mad!" cried the butcher as he pulled a cleaver from his bloody apron. The crowd muttered, and the butcher said, "If he is with you, he is not welcome here!"

James stepped between Jesus and the volatile mob to recount the night's events.

The blacksmith cut him off. "Your Jesus has no regard for our property," he sneered. "Get out of here!"

The angry crowd pleaded, "Go! You've done enough here already."

A different source of anger simmered inside him. How many years had they tried to bind him up and set guards over him? How long had he terrified them with his shrieks and tortured travelers? Today he spoke with his own voice. He reasoned and explained, but the change terrified them more than his violence.

The last piece of fish blackened, and the coals turned white. The crowd surrounded Jesus and his men hovering around the cooling embers. "Get out or we'll drive you out!" Chains rattled again, and rods thumped the ground.

"We will go," Jesus answered. He waved an arm to his men and directed them to the boats. The one called Peter draped the net over his shoulder and headed for the boats while the others kicked wet sand into the coals.

The man stood and backed away from the mob,

hoping not to startle the blacksmith. He waded into the water behind Jesus. This cliff full of tombs was no home. He couldn't stay and didn't want to. With Jesus there was power, provision, and belonging.

He waited his turn to climb in. As he reached for the boat's ledge, Jesus shook his head. "Where I am going, you cannot go."

"Please...please take me with you," he pleaded. He pointed to the tradesmen arguing about what could be salvaged from the sea. "They...please...please let me go with you. Look at them! They hate me!"

"They do not know me. But you know me."

He begged again, "Please, I will serve alongside you. I will do whatever you ask!"

"Good. Now, go home to your family."

Family? He'd forgotten. Would they recognize him? If they did, would they want him? "But what if—" he began.

"Tell them how much God has done for you today and how God had mercy on you. Tell them what I have made you. Trust me, friend."

Jesus reclined in the stern. The man let his hand drop from the boat's ledge. Peter and James shoved their vessels into the lake.

Assured of Jesus' departure, the entire crowd had migrated to the spectacle of bloating swine. Dragging some to land for butchering and engrossed in calculating losses, they argued and swore.

His borrowed cloak hung wet and heavy. Cold water numbed his legs. As Jesus and his men rowed away, he waded to shore. *Go home.* It wasn't far. He would knock at the door and wait patiently to be allowed in. There'd be no screaming, no doors ripped from hinges, no pottery thrown against the walls. He would show them he'd been set free, and he'd tell of the Most High God who liberates.

Boats bobbed westward, no bigger than a couple ducklings from where he stood. A broken iron manacle lay rusting at the water's edge as he slipped away to obey his Savior.

Drastic Deliverance

This was a horror scene, a nightmare the dreamer can't forget. But this was no dream. It was an ugly reality. Beyond the grotesque details given to us by traumatized witnesses, one astonishing reality stands out. Jesus left an enthralled congregation and traveled to the fetid tombs of Gadara to rescue one hopeless man from the talons of demon possession.*

The battle lines between the kingdom of God and the kingdom of the devil were drawn in a showdown over the territory of a man. A legion of evil set on destruction opposed the One who is Light and Life. The Son of God arrived on the eastern shore of the Sea of Galilee to destroy the devil's work.†

The Mystery of Absence and Presence

In his first lucid moments, this man was transformed. Normally he roamed, but suddenly he found himself seated at Jesus' feet. He used to live naked among the dead, but he discovered he'd been clothed. Jesus was the undeniable agent of this drastic end of misery. His arrival, command, and generous miracle precipitated such radical change that the man could not bear to let Jesus out of his sight.

Like a frightened child whose father must leave for

---

* Matthew's Gospel mentions two men. See Matthew 8:28.
† 1 John 3:8

work, this man stretched his arms upward for safety and begged to be taken along. His hope was in Jesus. His longing was the response of a soul plucked from hopelessness. He held no affection for his former life, and if he had known the words of our Sunday school songs, he might have sung, "No turning back, no turning back."

We have the urge to applaud him for wanting to be with Jesus. We recall another transformation, when blind Bartimaeus was healed and followed Jesus on the road.* The holy instinct of these men was to follow Jesus immediately.

So it comes as a shock to read, "As Jesus was getting into the boat, the man who had been demon-possessed begged to go with him. Jesus did not let him."† Despite pleading, tears, and maybe an account of what he feared might happen when Jesus left, "Jesus sent him away."‡

With furrowed brows and mouths agape, we empathize with the disappointed new believer because we want him to be with Jesus, too. What better place for

---

* See Mark 10:46–52.
† Mark 1:19
‡ Luke 8:38

a rescued soul to flourish than in the presence of Jesus and with the support of his disciples?

Alexander MacLaren writes, "Strange that Jesus should put aside a hand that sought to grasp His in order to be safe; but His refusal was, as always, the gift of something better, and He ever disappoints the wish in order more truly to satisfy the need."[4]

This man's story points to a promise Jesus made at the end of his earthly ministry. He told his baffled disciples, "It is best for you that I go away, because if I don't, the Advocate [Holy Spirit] won't come. If I do go away, then I will send him to you."* His disciples could not make sense of it, and before he physically departed, he assured them again, "I am with you always, to the very end of the age."†

An earthly father can console his child with warm promises of his return, but Jesus promises his uninterrupted presence. Like all of us, this man needed the supernatural presence of the Holy Spirit to accomplish the mission Jesus assigned him. The deliverer departed but the deliverance stayed, and at some

---

* John 16:7 (NLT)
† Matthew 28:20

unrecorded moment the presence of the Holy Spirit empowered him to go and tell.

Concentric Circles of Ministry

Demons had driven him into isolation among the dead, but Jesus sent him home to the living. His family, who had likely witnessed his decline and his twisted cravings, would be the first to ask, "What on earth happened?" With that invitation, this man had the joy of obeying his Savior and reporting how much the Lord had done for him.*

"Nothing was so likely to confirm and steady the convalescent mind as to dwell on the fact of his deliverance. Therefore he is sent to proclaim it to friends who had known his dreadful state, and amidst old associations which would help him to knit his new life to his old, and to treat his misery as a parenthesis."[5] As he traded in the market and sought a job, he'd wave to old and new friends, and the loose sleeves of his cloak would fall back to his elbows, revealing a web of scars—a testament to the end of misery.

---

* See Mark 5:19 .

His testimony points to Jesus' instruction to the disciples before he left them. Jesus informed his disciples they would be his witnesses first in their hometowns, then in neighboring towns, then in the entire region, and finally to the ends of the world.* It is the natural progression of ministry for a believer who's been radically transformed by Christ.

His life was such a holy spectacle that he eventually shared his story in the Decapolis—a region made up of ten cities, including Damascus, where a few years later a community of frightened believers would await the arrival of a different kind of madman (Saul), who would also meet Jesus on the road and be transformed.

Disappointed Wishes, Satisfied Needs

We are no strangers to disappointment in what we perceive to be good and holy plans. Our families and churches are filled with stories of vocations rerouted, ministries upended, and plans gone haywire. With the help of time and distance, we sometimes get the

---

* See Acts 1:8.

opportunity to reflect and find that disappointed wishes were God's way of satisfying our needs and building his kingdom. If we look carefully, we might see glimpses of a fisherman who ended up fishing for men.

Author Ken Gire recounts his short tenure as a pastor. He took the job because it was available and he was a seminary graduate. It was the reasonable course of action and certainly what everyone thought he should do. But after two years of pastoral awkwardness, he felt compelled to write a children's book. He found the project refreshing, satisfying, and fun. "And I felt guilty about that," Gire writes. "Not guilty for enjoying writing so much—guilty for enjoying the pastoring so little."[6] Several hundred thousand copies later, it is clear his ministry was not as a pastor but as a writer.

Sometimes, though, the results of a change in plans don't produce measurable, exponential results. God also delights to orchestrate his work in the hidden corners of an individual's heart.

Consider the Christian who is deeply invested in a demanding ministry. Her work is directly to and for Jesus, and she is intent on living "a life worthy of the calling."* But too soon the work becomes exhausting.

---

* Ephesians 4:1

Drained of enthusiasm for God's work—even dreading it—a Christian can crash and burn. We can be easily sidelined from ministry and bombarded with feelings of failure. But God tends to the weary soul with the refreshment of his kindness, saying, "I have made you worthy. I am not ashamed of the work I'm completing in you."

When we cannot see the path from start to finish, we may begrudge the whiplash of a course correction. He is the God of hope who enlivens us to follow and obey him even as he reserves the right to change our course.

The apostle Paul prays, "May the God of hope fill you with all joy and peace as you trust in him, so that you may overflow with hope by the power of the Holy Spirit."* Our hope is the secured certainty that Jesus is present in every dizzying disappointment. As we trust him, we will find *he* does not disappoint. He sets us on the course he always intended for his kingdom and his glory. As his trusting children, we get a front-row seat to his wild and surprising plan, which unfolds exactly as he knew it would.

---

* Romans 15:13

—

Dear Lord,

I am wowed by the power and authority you wield, but I confess I am more devoted to my intentions than to the needs you are addressing in me.

Lord, when you disappoint my wishes to satisfy my actual need, it feels harsh. Help me hold my plans loosely, offering them to you to conform and correct according to your will. Comfort me with the promise of your presence, especially when I feel disappointed.

Give me joy as I praise you for wherever you put me, and let me delight to tell the story of how you brought me there.

Despairing Hope

Jairus, Father of a Dying Daughter

When Jesus had again crossed over by boat to
the other side of the lake, a large crowd gathered
around him while he was by the lake. Then one of
the synagogue leaders, named Jairus, came, and
when he saw Jesus, he fell at his feet. He pleaded
earnestly with him, "My little daughter is dying.
Please come and put your hands on her so that
she will be healed and live." So Jesus went with
him. A large crowd followed and pressed around
him.....

While Jesus was still speaking, some people came
from the house of Jairus, the synagogue leader.
"Your daughter is dead," they said. "Why bother the
teacher anymore?"

Overhearing what they said, Jesus told him,
"Don't be afraid; just believe."

He did not let anyone follow him except Peter, James and John the brother of James. When they came to the home of the synagogue leader, Jesus saw a commotion, with people crying and wailing loudly. He went in and said to them, "Why all this commotion and wailing? The child is not dead but asleep." But they laughed at him.

After he put them all out, he took the child's father and mother and the disciples who were with him, and went in where the child was. He took her by the hand and said to her, *"Talitha koum!"* (which means "Little girl, I say to you, get up!"). Immediately the girl stood up and began to walk around (she was twelve years old). At this they were completely astonished. He gave strict orders not to let anyone know about this, and told them to give her something to eat.

—Mark 5:21–25, 35–43

Parallel Passages: Luke 8:40–56, Matthew 9:18–26

Leftover humidity from last night's storm had left the synagogue door swollen and stuck. Jairus shoved a shoulder against the damp wood. The door flew open and revealed what he'd feared. Wind had driven rain through a seam in the stone wall. A tiny river staggered across the floor. It followed the lowest seams in the tiles and collected in the sagging center of the synagogue. The podium stood in the expanding puddle.

Jairus sighed. Tension crawled from his shoulders toward his head. The water was an irritating trifle today. But if he didn't clean it up before the synagogue boys arrived, they'd be stomping in it at every opportunity—or wishing they could.

He grabbed a broom and with forceful strokes swept water from the podium toward the door.

Last Sabbath he'd stood in this spot, when it had been dry, and handed the scroll to the reader. The wooden spools had clunked against the stand, and the parchment had crackled as he unrolled it.

Jairus had scanned the congregation as he retreated from the podium to the entrance. Capernaum's devout were seated on three long stairs that ran the perimeter of the room. Directly in front of the reader were religious leaders visiting from Jerusalem. Their long-tasseled robes flowed from their shoulders and ornamented the floor. Along the next wall sat servants of the town's leading centurion. Rome set reminders of its rule in every outlying city, and Capernaum was no exception. But the centurion was good and had helped build this synagogue. He was not in attendance today, but some of his servants were.

Along the next wall, a mother whispered in her toddler's ear. He strained to escape and reached for the pillar in front of them. Pent-up energy danced in his eyes. While the mother wrestled the boy, his big sister patted and hushed a newborn.

Around the corner from that commotion sat Jairus' family. His daughter leaned against her mother. It was sweet and strange. At twelve, she was nearly the age of betrothal. In another year she'd be considered an adult. But slumped against her mother with her eyes closed, she was a sleepy child. His face flushed, and he glanced over to the leaders from Jerusalem to see if they had noticed.

The spools of the scroll thumped together as it rolled closed. The reading was over, and he hadn't quite heard it. He received the scroll and led the congregation in the creed.

"Hear, O Israel: The LORD our God, the LORD is one. Love the LORD your God with all your heart and with all your soul and with all your strength."*

---

* Deuteronomy 6:4–5

Glancing at his wife, he waited for her to rouse their daughter to join in as she should. Instead his wife stroked the girl's hair and only mouthed every few words of the creed. He stared to catch her eye and hoped the chorus of voices would wake his daughter. Instead, her head dropped forward as if she were exhausted by the admonition to love the Lord.

"Impress these commands on your children," the congregation continued. He dropped his gaze to the floor. They finished the recital with a benediction, and, family by family, the synagogue emptied.

"Peace to you, Jairus," the last parishioner called as he headed for home.

"May the Lord bless and keep you!" Jairus called after him.

"Jairus!" Inside the synagogue, his wife shouted.

Irritated, he went back in. Their daughter lay crumpled on the floor, his wife kneeling beside her. Jairus rushed to her side.

"Jairus, she doesn't wake!" All his irritation melted into fear. "Let's get her home." He scooped her from the floor. Her head fell back over his left arm, and her legs dangled limp over his right. Heat from her neck burned through the sleeve of his cloak.

—

Rainwater from the roof continued to puddle at the center of the synagogue like a dirty glass discarded on the floor. He caught a glimpse of his rippled reflection. His face was drawn and ashen, a testament to the heartbreak. He swept the reflection out the door and flung it into the courtyard. It spattered the stairs and evaporated under the morning sun.

Any moment, the young Jewish boys of Capernaum would trickle in for their Hebrew lessons. He shielded his eyes as he waited. Below him a crowd gathered at the shoreline to welcome two fishing boats. But they did not unload a fresh catch, and the people were not gathered to buy fish.

Like grapes in a winepress, the citizens of Capernaum bumped into one another on the shore. Contained by the sea on one side and the booths of the market on the other, they pressed toward the man at the center. Jesus had returned.

Months ago, Jairus had invited Jesus to teach in the synagogue, and the congregation had been amazed. Jesus did not speculate about what the prophets meant. He taught with authority. Whenever he was in town, the synagogue was full.

But it wasn't only his teaching that drew the crowds. One Sabbath Jesus singled out a parishioner with a crippled hand and pointed to his mangled fingers. "Stretch it out," he said. Immediately the man could straighten and curl his fingers.

Jairus smiled. He was glad Jesus had returned.

"Sir!" A young student about seven years of age came barreling down the road, splashing through puddles strewn about the street.

"You're not late, Jacob," Jairus called.

"Sir," he panted, "your daughter…"

Jairus dropped the broom and pointed the boy into the synagogue, where the Hebrew teacher waited. He ran the short distance to his home. A woman dressed in black closed the gate to his courtyard as she left. The city's mourners had been put on notice, but their services were not yet needed.

He slammed open the door and a household servant stepped out of the way as Jairus rushed to his daughter's bedroom. His wife knelt by the bed. Beside her lay a soaked rag in an empty bowl. When he entered, she burst into tears.

"I don't know what to do for her, Jairus."

Jairus knelt beside her. His daughter's face was rimmed by wet tendrils of black hair stuck to her skin. Her lips appeared as shriveled and purple as a forgotten fig. Jairus leaned in to kiss her, and as he did, a small breath left her lips. It smelled of decay.

Jairus covered his mouth to muffle an eruption of fear.

"Jairus…" his wife pleaded.

"Jesus is back," he said, wiping his eyes. He kissed her and left the room.

"Refill the water," he instructed as he passed his household servant.

"Yes, sir."

~

Jairus raced from the house and overcame the mourner he'd seen. He rounded the corner onto the street that led to the seaside market. Weaving through the tax collectors' booths and the vendors, he merged with the mass of citizens swarming Jesus. Most of Capernaum had descended upon the beach. Jairus smoothed his sleeves, dabbed sweat from his brow, and pushed into the jostling crowd.

"Jairus!" a neighbor called. "He's returned!"

"Yes," replied Jairus as he pushed past the man. "Excuse me."

"Jairus, it looks like your teacher will be back in town for the Sabbath," said another.

Jairus nodded. "Jesus!" he called above the din.

The group stalled and parted the way for him. He ran toward Jesus and fell to his knees in the sand. "Please," he panted, and swallowed. "My only daughter . . . please come to my house and put your hands on her so she will be healed because"—he paused—"she is dying." Saying it aloud hurt.

"I will go to your house," Jesus said.

Jairus scrambled to his feet, his hope buoyed by Jesus' quick agreement. He was no longer running, but his breath was fast and shallow. *A few moments, darling. Jesus is coming.*

Jairus found himself two paces in front of Jesus, then three. He was a bridled warhorse with an instinct to race home but reined in by this giddy mob. He waited, resisting the urge to grab Jesus' arm and drag him away. Jairus waited as the crowd crawled along. They had finally made it from the beach to the main street of Capernaum. From here Jairus could see the corner of his block. It was not far, but at this pace they might as well be walking to Jerusalem. As Jairus was ready to demand that Jesus hurry, Jesus stopped. "Who touched me?" he asked.

The crushing crowd halted. Jesus glanced over one shoulder, then the other. His disciples muttered to one another in confusion.

Jairus' heart banged in his chest. He calculated the short distance to his house as one of Jesus' disciples voiced what Jairus had been thinking. "How can you ask such a thing? Everyone's touching you! Look at them!"

"This was different," he said. "I felt power go out of me."

It sounded absurd, but it was the same power Jairus hoped for for his daughter. *Hurry with your power, Jesus!* But Jesus kept scanning the faces.

"Please…" Jairus began. His voice cracked. "I'm sure it was…" But Jesus didn't respond, and Jairus' words drowned in the chaos of questions and pointing fingers.

From somewhere behind the skirts and cloaks a woman's cry erupted. "It was me!" She flung herself down in front of Jesus. Hunched, with her garment spread behind her, faint blood stains whispered her sickness. Like ripples running from a dropped rock, the people receded from this unclean woman.

Jairus recognized her at once. She'd been sick for as long as his little girl had been alive. She had plied him for help in retaining physicians and treatments from Jerusalem and Tyre. Nothing had worked.

Oh, not today. At once he was ashamed for his silent cruelty and frightened by the delay. Jairus shook like a dried leaf fastened to its branch by a thin stem of hope.

"I knew if I touched your clothes..." she began. Everyone hushed as this wisp of a woman recounted twelve years of suffering and failed remedies.

Her face was flushed and polished with tears. When she finally paused for breath, Jairus thought she might be done. He stepped toward Jesus to usher him away, but she prattled on. Jesus was stuck in the mud of this throng, and the urgency of a dying daughter couldn't pull him out.

Jairus wove through those standing between Jesus and his house, asking them to step aside. "Please, Jesus will need to pass through quickly, so..." He was sweeping the air in front of him with both arms as he parted them and returned to get Jesus.

"Daughter," Jesus said, and Jairus turned to ask Peter to keep the path clear.

As he opened his mouth, a voice whispered behind him, "Jairus."

A somber-faced household servant beckoned him to the outskirts of the crowd. Jairus shook his head. *No. No. No.* The servant slipped an arm around Jairus' shoulder and turned him away from Jesus. He spoke in a low voice. "Your daughter is dead."

Jairus might as well have been stabbed. The sea breeze was too thick. He couldn't catch his breath. He doubled over, and the street stones twirled beneath him. He saw the woman on the ground smiling. Jesus leaned forward to help her stand.

His servant squeezed his forearm, urging him to leave. "Come now, Jairus. Let's not bother the teacher anymore."

Jesus turned from the woman and faced Jairus without regret or apology, but Jairus had no words. *Hurry* was irrelevant. *Please* had not helped. Jairus had failed his family, and Jesus had failed him.

"Don't be afraid, Jairus. Keep on believing."

Jairus blinked. Jesus spoke as if the delay did not matter, as if there were no cause for concern, as if he'd been strolling on the beach and had the pleasure of visiting a friend on the way. Despair socked Jairus in the throat. He was still gasping for breath.

Jesus extended an arm to Jairus and his servant. "Coming?"

—

He heard it before he could see it. Flutes wailed shrill tunes he recognized but did not love. Tiny cymbals clinked a slow rhythm, as if taking over for a heart that had ceased to beat. Above the sad song, the forced wailing of women dutifully demanded everyone within earshot join the mourning. The commotion confirmed the worst.

As they turned the corner to Jairus' house, the funeral proceedings came into view. Ash had been flung upward, an outward sign of inward grief. It littered the air and settled on black garments. The large group of mourners knelt and paced, bowed and stood—a visual rendering of the havoc in his chest. Neighbors filed in and out of the house, stirred to a frenzy of sadness. Outside the door lay a basket of woven reeds long enough to carry the body of a girl.

It was a miserable but familiar scene. He'd witnessed it many times, but never at his own house.

Jesus spoke to his disciples. "Peter, James, and

John, you come with us. The rest of you, stay out here with the people. Encourage them while we go inside."

Jairus stopped. Perhaps if he too stayed outside this dreadful announcement would go away. A neighbor woman waddled through the door jostling a steaming pot of soup. The aroma of vegetable broth and roasted lamb turned his stomach. Jesus put an arm around Jairus' shoulder, and Jairus heard it again: "Don't be afraid. Just believe."

Inside his house, the air was humid with tears and sweat. The comforts of home had been sucked out of the room and replaced with unfamiliarity. Cries echoed and swirled around him as if they were bouncing around the circumference of a damp well. Jairus stifled the urge to cover his ears and close his eyes. He wanted to hold his wife and see his sweet girl before she was carried away.

"Why all this commotion? Stop wailing!" Jesus shouted over the cries. Jairus started. Mourning women opened their eyes and closed their mouths— a moment of respite from the noise. Jairus' wife appeared in the main room, her eyes nearly swelled shut and her outer garment ripped from the neck to her waist. Lingering ash stuck to her tear-streaked cheeks. On seeing Jairus, she pushed aside her company, fell into his arms, and sobbed.

"Teacher…" The chief mourner began to make her case. "By what authority do you suggest we dispense with propriety and tradition? We are here to comfort the family, after all."

Jairus listened to her protest but had no will to argue. Grief commanded his full attention until Jesus answered her objections.

"The girl is not dead but asleep."

She huffed—a laugh disguised as an exhale.

"What did he say?" asked a woman in the far corner.

"He said she's only sleeping," she called over her shoulder. Scornful muttering erupted.

She strode toward Jesus, prepared for confrontation, but stopped in front of Jairus and spat, "I guess we are not needed if she's only sleeping!" She waited for Jairus to beg them to stay—to honor his daughter with cries and to invite the community into his misery. But two words bounding around his mind stopped him. *Just believe.*

She whisked up her skirts and marched out with her exasperated band of lamenters tagging behind.

Musicians and neighbors remained, unsure of what had occurred. "All of you, go outside!" Jesus said. They left to join the offended mourners. Walls muffled the ridicule outside as word passed from mourner to neighbor that his daughter merely slept. Jairus froze, paralyzed by shock and grief.

"Come on in," Jesus said, and led the parents and three of his disciples into the girl's room.

Jairus' daughter lay stretched on a wooden plank for ease of transport. She might have been a statue except for the blood drying at the corners of her mouth. Pallid skin sagged in the hollows of her cheeks. Her brittle hair, now smoothed toward the floor, was crowned with a wreath of flowering myrtle, the last vestige of life. Someone had draped linen over her legs and crossed her arms upon her chest as though she clutched her broken heart.

Jairus trembled and leaned into the wall to support himself and the weight of his wife. Tears seeped into his mouth as he whispered from the psalms, "You have made her days a mere handbreadth."*

He searched Jesus' face for an explanation. Jesus knelt beside the girl. His dusty robe splayed before

---

* Psalm 39:5

him. Curling his fingers around her fragile hand, he lifted it from her chest. As if summoning her from the next room, he called, "Little girl, get up!"

Sound fell away save for a rushing in Jairus' ears.

Under the linen sheet, her toes flexed toward the ceiling as though stretching after a nap. Her eyelids, a moment ago sealed like wax, fluttered. Her knees drew upward, and Jesus supported her back as she sat up. As Jesus stood, so did she. The linen sheet fell around her feet. Holding Jesus' hand, she steadied herself and kicked it off.

Jairus and his wife gasped and lunged toward her, wrapping her warm body between them. His wife pressed her mouth to the girl's cheek, kissing and stammering, "My...my little girl." Jairus held her hands and pulled back to study her at arm's length. Her lips were colored like pomegranates, and her cheeks were flushed as if she'd spent the day in sunshine.

Jesus smiled with the same leisurely kindness he's shown the woman in the road. Three bewildered disciples stood shoulder to shoulder, unmoving, faces pale with astonishment. Jairus' wife cried happily, stroking her daughter's hair, drawing a finger along her cheek, squeezing her hands, and repeating, "My girl. My sweet little girl."

"Jairus." Jesus' solemn tone demanded attention. "I must be clear with you," he said. "You must not let anyone know about this."

Jairus nodded furiously.

"Don't tell anyone what happened in here."

Jairus' wife dabbed her eyes with her headscarf, mystified but mumbling agreement. "Yes. Certainly. We will do whatever you say."

"Good. Now, why don't you give her something to eat," Jesus said.

Jairus' wife threw both hands in the air and shook her head in alarm. "Of course!" She laced her daughter's arm through her own and ushered her to the kitchen. "Darling, let's get you some food. All of you, come and eat!"

The kitchen was piled with tokens of sympathy, untouched—fruit, baked fish, and that pot of soup, still steaming.

She laughed and said, "Our table is full, darling! What would you like first?"

Dizzy with wonder, Jairus stared at Jesus.

Israel's rightful king, in his home, had called his daughter back from the regions of the dead, and Jairus could only stare. *Prophet? Teacher? Fraud?* Synagogue men had debated, but Jairus knew. *Jesus is the Messiah, the Christ of God.*

Knowing Jesus

Opinions about Jesus were varied and strongly held. He was accused of lunacy and lauded as wonderful. His enemies dubbed him a devil, and his disciples confessed him as the Son of God. But if there was one point they agreed upon, it was that Jesus was unpredictable.

Jairus had a distinct advantage over many at that time because much of Jesus' ministry took place in Capernaum. Though Jesus didn't own a home there, it served as a home base. To Jairus, Jesus wasn't some distant troublemaker. He was a neighbor.

Within the space of a year or so, Jairus had been introduced to Jesus, invited him to speak at his synagogue, marveled as he preached with authority, and watched him exorcize a possessed parishioner.

Besides what he personally witnessed, he'd heard accounts from around town. A formerly paralyzed man hauled his stretcher down the street. The centurion, who had helped to build Jairus' synagogue, reported that his most trusted servant was healed with a word. In the nearby town of Nain, a young man being carried to a grave on his burial plank sat up at Jesus' touch.

Whether people heard the stories as firsthand testimony or the tales of bored orators, the accounts spread like wildfire across the region. Miraculous accounts couldn't be suffocated, only disbelieved.

Jairus believed. He had every reason to expect with certainty that Jesus could heal his dying daughter. In his desperation, he rushed his emergency to Jesus.

We feel for Jairus. We have seen Jesus intervene, and we depend on his ability to come through again. In our emergencies, we have rushed the throne of grace with prayers that fly from terrified lips. The second before an airbag deploys, the moment after a diagnosis is declared, as we are drowning in waves of tragedy, an immediate crystal clarity presents: our only hope is Jesus. We're so sure of it, we pray leading prayers. "Lord, protect me! Heal her! Remove these trials!"

He can, but sometimes he does not. On occasion we find ourselves, like Jairus, within arm's length of our powerful Savior as we swallow the worst possible news. The crowd churns in slow motion, and the racket of surrounding voices is muted by one repeated line: "Don't bother him. It's too late."

A Surprising Grace

We suppose God has failed. We have prayed and pleaded, offering suggestions as if God were bound to our short multiple-choice form of possible solutions. When expectations go unmet, it appears he has chosen "none of the above."

Pastor and author John Koessler refers to disappointment as a "surprising grace."[7] When we find Christ's unexpected work blooming on the dead branch of disappointment, we can receive it as undeserved favor—a grace.

Disappointment is often the pivot point where we stop trying to lead Jesus and start following his lead. With the ropes of expectation cut, we are relieved of the burden of dragging Jesus at a snail's pace to our own destination—our way, our timeline, by the methods we prefer, to accomplish the results we desire. Without the fetters of prescribed results, we are free to observe the glories of Christ. When the tension goes slack, Jesus offers encouragement: "Don't be afraid. Keep on believing."

In shocked silence, we—like Jairus—show ourselves to be kin to Abraham. "Even when there was no reason for hope, Abraham kept hoping."* It wasn't blind hope. It wasn't self-willed telekinetic energy or the furious concentration of a mind trick. Abraham hoped because God had promised. Jairus hoped because Jesus told him to keep at it, and we hope because we serve the same Lord, who does not change.

Witness the Glory of God

Jairus became a silent follower, going down the street, into the house, which Jesus cleared in a slightly less dramatic fashion than he had cleared the money changers from the temple. Jesus "took the child's father and mother" to the private room where he displayed his power and glory. From the mouth of Jesus, the ordinary words "Little girl, arise!" express his

---

* Romans 4:18 (NLT)

authority over fatal devastation. A little group of six witnesses experience the glory of God.

More Than We Ask or Think

Jesus has reserved the glory of bodily resurrection for those years of his earthly ministry and for his future return. In the meantime, we can observe the glories of the resurrected Christ even as we endure devastation.

A striking example is told in the missionary memoir of Darlene Deibler Rose. During the terrors of World War II, she was interned in New Guinea in a Japanese prison camp, where she was interrogated, tortured, falsely convicted of espionage, sentenced to beheading, and held in a cell on death row.

One day, through a window near the top of her cell, she observed another prisoner in the courtyard receive a bundle of bananas from someone outside the prison fence.

She spent the rest of that day wobbling between faith and doubt. She wrestled with her thoughts, concocted plans for how the Lord might bring her a banana, and finally prayed, "Lord, there's no one here who could get a banana to me. There's no way for You to do it. Please don't think I'm not thankful for the rice porridge. It's just that—well, those bananas looked so delicious!"[8]

The next day all prisoners were made to perform their bowing rituals. Despite their weakened state, they were beaten for every violation of a perfect ninety-degree bow. Back in her cell, she heard the ominous clicking of an officer's shoes and dreaded having to stand and bow once more. She prayed for strength. When the cell door opened, an officer with whom she had previously shared Christ stood smiling at her. In her shock, she exclaimed it was like seeing an old friend.

He acknowledged her poor health and left. When the door closed, she realized she had not bowed at all and began to panic. When she heard the officer returning, she prepared for bowing and for a beating.

But when he opened the door, he laid a gift on the cell floor: ninety-two bananas. She writes: "I pushed the bananas into a corner and wept before Him. 'Lord, forgive me; I'm so ashamed. I couldn't trust You enough to get even one banana for me. Just look at them—there are almost a hundred.' In the quiet of the shadowed cell, He answered back within my heart: *'That's what I delight to do, the exceeding abundant above anything you ask or think.'* "[9]

On the day she "peeled the black, shriveled skin from the last banana,"[10] she was, in a terrifying and miraculous manner, delivered from death row and returned to her barracks and her friends. Her troubles were far from over, but she was convinced of God's power and willingness to provide more than she imagined was possible.

In the Absence of Praise Songs

When we catch glimpses of the glories of Christ, stunned silence can be an appropriate response. The Gospel writers record no rejoicing or praise songs after the girl was raised. Instead, Jairus and his wife are described as "overcome with amazement" (ESV) or "astonished with great astonishment" (KJV). The original Greek word, *existémi*, implies that they were "beside themselves." It speaks of a kind of gasping shock and wonder that requires Jesus to remind them to feed their daughter, who had probably not eaten in quite some time.

The humbling glory of God reminds us that we are small children in the hands of a powerful Father.

Sometimes we hope for less than Jesus offers, and sometimes he offers more than we dared to ask.

~

Dear Lord,

I confess, I am offended by your unpredictability. I operate under the illusion I can control your action with my good decisions. But you do not act as I expect. I've brought emergencies, and you have delayed. I begrudge your timing and your inaction.

Forgive me for doubting your holy plan. I acknowledge that I cannot see the whole picture. I can hardly perceive my own heart.

When I find myself at the devastating crossroads of disappointment, turn me toward you. Give me the wisdom to follow. Open my eyes to your glory so that my complaints are silenced and my soul is filled with awe.

Delayed Hope

Martha, Mary, and Lazarus

Now a man named Lazarus was sick. He was from Bethany, the village of Mary and her sister Martha. (This Mary, whose brother Lazarus now lay sick, was the same one who poured perfume on the Lord and wiped his feet with her hair.) So the sisters sent word to Jesus, "Lord, the one you love is sick."

When he heard this, Jesus said, "This sickness will not end in death. No, it is for God's glory so that God's Son may be glorified through it." Now Jesus loved Martha and her sister and Lazarus. So when he heard that Lazarus was sick, he stayed where he was two more days, and then he said to his disciples, "Let us go back to Judea." . . .

On his arrival, Jesus found that Lazarus had already been in the tomb for four days.

—John 11:1–6, 17

The afternoon breeze blew dust through the front door, and Martha choked on it. She wiped her mouth and eyes with her scarf and fumbled with the strings of her purse.

The young man in the doorway shifted his weight from one foot to the other. His arms glistened with perspiration, and his feet were crusted in two days of dirt.

Martha thought to invite him in to wash, but the house was already full. A company of traditional mourners, whose duty was to alert the town of the recent death, had stationed themselves around her house, wailing and groaning. The cacophony was also an attempted courtesy to drown out the cries of the bereft family.

"Mary," Martha called to her sister above the noise. Mary joined her in the doorway. "Where has the wash basin gone?"

Mary glanced around the entry. "Perhaps someone used it in preparing the body for burial," she whispered. "I'll go see."

Martha turned her attention back to the young man. "Five pieces?" she asked, digging for coins at the bottom of her bag.

"Yes. That's what you promised on my return."

Martha cinched her purse strings and clutched five silver coins. Mary hovered at her shoulder and whispered, "It's in use." Martha shook her stare from his dirty feet and let the impulse go.

A bead of sweat dripped from his jawline, and Martha turned her attention back to business. "Was that all he said?" she asked. With the cheerless flutes piping out sadness and a chorus of wailing filling the house, Martha hoped she had misunderstood.

"Yes. That was all." He repeated the message: "'This sickness will not end in death. It is for God's glory so that God's Son may be glorified through it.'"

Mary exhaled and started to cry again. Martha pulled her close and kissed the top of her head. The messenger dropped his head and stepped back from the doorway, his distance an act of reverence for their grief.

Martha waved for him to come back. She let the coins drop into his hand one at a time, clinking as they counted themselves. He hesitated and opened his mouth as if he might ask a question but then thought better of it. Bowing, he dismissed himself. Martha wouldn't have begrudged his question. He was the messenger of a happy promise of life delivered to a funeral. The discrepancy rattled in her heart.

—

As the sun crept behind the Mount of Olives, Martha's house rested in its shadow. With hugs and promises to pray, friends and relatives from Jerusalem returned home. A few visitors stayed with neighbors, and several had retired to Martha's guest room.

That morning Martha had found Lazarus still as a stone, and by afternoon he was entombed behind one.

She'd stood by as mourners laid him in this room and prepared him for burial. They had washed, wrapped, and anointed his body with spices and aloe. The room still smelled of myrrh, and the floor was speckled with drops of oil. According to custom, the furniture was toppled and the chairs were upturned. In the dim light of a flickering lamp, their shadows quivered on the walls, a telling symbol of the upheaval in her heart. Mary sat beside her on the floor, knees hugged to her chest, head resting on Martha's shoulder.

Mary inhaled a choppy breath and whispered, "If Jesus had been here, Lazarus wouldn't have died."

"I know," Martha replied. She leaned close and rested her head on Mary's shoulder. "I keep wondering if it was Jesus who got the message"—she hesitated to state the obvious—"because the message was wrong."

Martha had spent the morning trying to sort it out. Had their messenger found the right person? The reply sounded like Jesus, but if it was from him, he was mistaken. Jesus could surprise and confound, but he had never been wrong.

Until today. Lazarus' sickness had ended in death.

"Do you think he'll come?" Mary asked.

"I think so." But Martha was not at all certain. Jesus knew how easily she worried, and he had healed so many in Galilee and Judea. Lazarus was his dear friend, not a Judean stranger. Martha couldn't reconcile it, unless someone other than Jesus had cruelly or mistakenly replied.

Mary nodded and closed her eyes. "We will see him when he comes for Passover."

Martha stood and extended her hands to help Mary up. They held each other, faces buried in each other's shoulders, softly shaking. Finally, Martha whispered, "Let's get some rest."

⁓

Four days after the worst day of her life, Martha sat on a stool tossing sticks into the cooking fire. She blew into the flame, and the wood began to crackle. To face the constant company, Martha needed solitude. Guests and mourners would come and go for a week, and this morning she wanted these dark, early moments to herself. The silence in her kitchen made room for the song in her heart, and she sang of hope in her grief: "In you, Lord, I have taken refuge; let me never be put to shame; deliver me in your righteousness. Turn your ear to me, come quickly to my rescue; be my rock of refuge, a strong fortress to save me."*

She bent toward the fire and heat warmed her face. Houseguests would soon wake. Friends and relatives from Jerusalem would arrive again today with tears and hugs, food and drink. Yesterday's gifts were still spread upon the table. A wrapped barley loaf lay

---

* Psalm 31:1–2

beside a clay pot with honey dripping down its sides. Three shriveled grapes dangled from a nearly naked stem. Busying herself in the kitchen wasn't necessary, but she put the water on the stove and grabbed a cloth to wipe up the honey.

By the time Martha had tidied the kitchen, Mary was hugging guests. They poured in, laying condolences on her table—boiled eggs, raisin cakes, a pot of stew. Martha whisked the stew from the table and set it on the stove to keep it warm.

"Martha!" Her cousin Joanna entered. "Leave this to me. Join your sister and receive your guests."

"Thank you," Martha said, and hugged her. Martha smoothed the tablecloth and centered it on the table. She tossed the grape stems in the fire as she backed out of the kitchen. As long as she was among the ingredients and dishes, she could distract herself with the quality of the wine and the texture of flour. She could smell the cheese and know whether the goats had grazed on flowers or bitter weeds. Surrounded by mourners, she would be pummeled with reminders that Lazarus was gone and Jesus had not come.

By afternoon the house was throbbing with too many bodies pressed inside too few walls. Steam from the kitchen and the smell of sweaty guests had overpowered the leftover aroma of myrrh. Again and again Martha detailed to her visitors the awful scene of finding Lazarus. They peppered her with questions. *How long had he been sick? Did the doctor say what caused it? Did you send word to your friend Jesus?*

After a particularly tearful recounting, Joanna rushed from the kitchen to embrace her. As they embraced, Joanna whispered, "Guests from Jerusalem saw Jesus and his disciples on the road. He is on his way."

Martha's throat tightened, and her heart bumped against it. She excused herself and followed Joanna into the kitchen. "I'm going to meet him," Martha said.

"Take someone with you," Joanna demanded. "You shouldn't be leaving!"

Martha glanced into the next room where Mary was surrounded by guests, recounting the tragedy. "He can't be far. I'll be back." With her head covered and her eyes down, Martha slipped out the door.

She rounded the curve in the road that led out of Bethany and toward Jerusalem. The Master's tasseled robe flapped in the breeze as they strolled, and his disciples hovered around him. Martha swallowed a cry before it left her throat. She wadded her skirts in her fists and ran to him. "Lord," she said, panting, "if you had been here my brother would not have died." The cry she had suppressed resurfaced. Wind whipped her hair and tangled it in her tears. "But I know that even now God will give you whatever you ask."

She flinched at her own audacity. A young girl in Capernaum, a widow's son in Nain, both brought back to life on the day of their death, and only because Jesus had been there. Had he not sent word that death would not be the end? A glimmer of the impossible flashed in her mind.

"Your brother will rise again," Jesus said.

She brushed wet wisps of hair off her cheeks and smoothed them under her scarf in vain, bracing for disappointment. Jesus was right. Lazarus would rise again. Someday. Someday they would march arm in arm into God's kingdom. Martha nodded in agreement, but the tears continued to fall. "I know he will rise again in the resurrection at the last day." A great chasm of time lay between that day and this one. She dropped her head, covered her face with her hands, and tasted the salt of grief.

"Martha." Jesus lifted her chin. "I am the resurrection and the life. Anyone who believes in me will live, even after dying. Everyone who lives in me and believes in me will never ever die." She nodded. "Do you believe this, Martha?"*

"Yes, Lord," she said. "I have always believed you are the Messiah, the Son of God, the one who has come into the world from God."†

"Why don't you go and get Mary and bring her here," said Jesus.

Martha obeyed. But when she and Mary left the house, many of the guests and mourners followed. When Mary saw Jesus, she ran. Martha squirmed in the uncomfortable gap between her grieving sister and the crowd she'd so quickly abandoned. She slowed, let Mary run ahead, and bridged the distance between Mary and the mourners who had come along to comfort her.

They whispered behind her. "There he is! They say he's healed blind men. Would it be too much trouble to heal a sick man?" Martha cringed. She was sorry she had not kept up with Mary. He was the Christ, and she knew it. But that exact question had slithered from her heart over the past few days.

Mary reached Jesus and crumpled into a sobbing

---

* John 11:25–26 (NLT)
† John 11:27 (NLT)

heap at his feet and cried, "Lord, if only you had been here, my brother would not have died." Martha felt heat rise in her cheeks as their sad conversation was laid bare before Jesus. Their shock and disappointment with him was in full view.

Mary's shoulders heaved as she gasped. The group who had followed joined Mary in her crying, partly to preserve her dignity but also to honor Lazarus. Despite tradition and their good intentions, Martha was weary of their racket.

Although the sun was high, a shiver rustled through Jesus, and his brow furrowed. Was it grief or anger? Martha could not tell.

"Where have you laid him?" Jesus asked.

"Come and see," Martha replied. As they climbed the dusty slope toward the tomb, he smeared tears into his beard.

He loved him, Martha thought. *He loves us all.* Her eyes stung and her head pounded.

They came to the hillside where, four days ago, many in this same crowd had carried Lazarus on a burial plank and laid him to rest on his final bed. On that day Mary and Martha had followed Lazarus' body as it was carried by mourning men. Today, they led Jesus, his disciples, and the mourners to his tomb.

Olive trees lined the paths in solemn rows. Their branches stretched high, with buds waiting to be summoned in season. A large stone had been pushed over the entrance to the cave, and in its center, an inscription read, "Lazarus rests in peace." Martha pointed Mary's attention to the epitaph. "Peace," Martha whispered.

"Peace for him," Mary replied, "but we still ache."

Martha opened her mouth to console her sister as Jesus turned to the men behind him and said, "Take away the stone."

Mary stood straight. One man stepped away from Jesus and nearly tripped over the line of stones bordering the path behind him. Martha flitted between Mary and Jesus, stuttering and trembling. "But Lord"—she grabbed his arm—"by now there is a bad odor! He's been there four days!"

Jesus shook his head. "Didn't I say that if you believed, you would see the glory of God?"

Martha went cold. She scanned the group. Women were wide-eyed and whispering. One man grumbled, "He should have come days ago if he wanted a farewell."

Jesus motioned toward the grave stone again. "Take it away."

Three men appointed themselves to the task and

the stone scraped from the opening of the tomb. Like a breeze carries mist, cool air carried familiar scents of myrrh mingled with the mildew of a damp cave. Martha covered her mouth and nose with her scarf.

Jesus gazed at the sky, past the tops of the olive trees, and prayed, "Father, I'm thankful you have heard me."

Martha stared into the sky where his gaze was fixed. In the opening between the branches, birds threaded in and out of thin clouds.

"I knew that you always hear me," Jesus said, "but I'm saying this for the benefit of these people standing here, that they may believe you sent me."

Martha felt the sting of her questions. *Why? When? Why not?* She believed and had said so.

But before she could reiterate her belief, Jesus stepped forward and shouted into the cave, "Lazarus, come out!"

Mary whimpered. Doves rushed from the branches above them. Inside the cave something rustled like a disoriented animal scuffling about an empty cistern. Pebbles tumbled out as though kicked.

A chill shot through Martha's limbs like lightning. She shivered, then froze. In the opening of the tomb stood the form of a man, strips of burial cloths hanging loose. Death unraveled. A burial shroud veiled his face as he stepped into the afternoon sun.

No one breathed.

"Take off the grave clothes and let him go," Jesus said.

Martha inched toward the figure and pulled the cloth from his face. She stumbled back, afraid to touch what might be a vision, fragile as a glistening bubble.

He extended his arm, bound in linen. Martha took the loose end between her thumb and finger and began to unwind it. Warmth radiated from his hand to hers.

He who believes in me will live.

I am the resurrection and the life.

Do you believe?

Lazarus blinked.

Martha grasped his hand, coursing with life, and witnessed the glory of God.

God of the Last-Minute Rescue

Some have called him "God of the eleventh hour," as if he shows up in the nick of time. He halted the knife of Abraham. He parted the Red Sea as a nation fled. He spared Rahab as her city crumbled around her.

Mary and Martha knew of this God.

But for the little family at Bethany, the eleventh hour had passed. Also the twelfth. When all hope was lost, Jesus employed grief, mourning, and tradition to gather an audience to witness his glory. With resurrection power, he proved the eleventh hour has no bearing on his ability.

Beloved Family

Martha and Mary are perhaps two of the most studied and well-known women in the Gospels. Every time we read about them, they were with Jesus. He was in their home in Bethany where Martha served and Mary sat and listened to him teach, showing herself to be a disciple. He was with them in their grief as they stood outside their brother's tomb. A short time later, he was the dinner guest when Mary "wasted" her perfume to honor him and prepare his body for burial.

In each setting we find the sisters comfortable with Jesus. Mary was enthralled with his teaching. Martha felt justified complaining to him. They agreed to send their urgent requests to Jesus, knowing he would understand the urgency of their vague message: "The one you love is sick."*

With this history of friendship, it is clear that "Jesus loved Martha and her sister and Lazarus."† Mary and Martha did not question his love. It was his love for them that supplied the courage to send their urgent news.

If they had known the words, Mary and Martha might have sung with the nineteenth-century hymn writer:

> *I must tell Jesus all of my trials;*
> *I cannot bear these burdens alone;*
> *In my distress He kindly will help me;*
> *He ever loves and cares for His own.*[11]

Assurance of his love multiplied hope.

A Loving Delay

When Jesus heard that the one he loved was sick, he knew it was Lazarus. We expect to hear, "So Jesus left

---

* John 11:3
† John 11:5

his ministry in the region of Perea and hurried to the home of Mary and Martha." Or at the very least we want to read, "Because of their trust and unwavering belief in his power, Jesus, who was a day's journey from their home, spoke the word and Lazarus was healed."

Instead we are shocked to find that "when he heard that Lazarus was sick, he stayed where he was two more days."*

Perhaps it was a mercy that Mary and Martha may have thought it was a miscommunication or their poor timing. In reality, Christ's delay was deliberate. Unbeknownst to any of the people standing outside the tomb, the too-late arrival of Jesus is for the unforgettable benefit of his beloved. He delayed and prayed to help their unbelief.† "Christ's delays are the delays of love."[12]

Martha had resigned herself to the idea that Lazarus would rise eventually, but not until the "last day," when all believers will rise to everlasting life. Though she knew God would grant Jesus whatever he asked, her utter alarm at opening the tomb gives us a clue that she was not expecting a resurrection on *this* day.

---

* John 11:6
† See John 11:42.

Inseparable Fear and Glory

Just when their hearts and minds are rife with confusion, resignation, and scorn, Jesus calls a dead man out of a tomb to live, and we get a glimpse of an arresting pattern throughout the Gospels. When Jesus reveals his glory, the witnesses are terrified.

As his disciples panted in a waterlogged boat, bobbing on the dissipating waves of a calm sea, "they were terrified."* When Jesus was found to be the cause of two thousand drowned swine and the restored sanity of a madman, the townspeople were "overcome with fear."† When his three closest disciples—Peter, James, and John—were privileged to see Jesus transfigured and hear God's audible voice, "they fell facedown to the ground, terrified."‡

Outside of Lazarus' tomb, with the breath sucked from their lungs, his witnesses fell deathly silent. Jesus shook the observers from their catatonic fear with the simple instruction, "Take off the grave clothes and let

---

* Mark 4:41
† Luke 8:37
‡ Matthew 17:6

him go."* Although they were not disappointed, they were dumbstruck with awe and wonder and probably terrified.

God's greatness humbles those who see it. The "fear of the Lord" generates wisdom in those who believe— the wisdom to marvel in silence, the wisdom to obey simple instructions, and the wisdom to trust our drastic God, who is prone to "delay" because he loves us.

A Disappointing Return

We would be remiss if we did not take a speculative peek at the shrouded face of Lazarus. The apostle Paul tells us that to be absent in the body is to be at home with the Lord.† Lazarus spent four days in the visible presence of God, free from sin, with a wide-eyed view to the inheritance that awaits believers. For Lazarus, that future hope was made a present possession for a moment of eternity. Lazarus, whose tears had been wiped by God, might now have been quivering with sadness underneath that "cloth around his

---

* John 11:44
† See 2 Corinthians 5:8 (NASB).

face"* as he stepped out of the glories of heaven and into the comparatively dim light of earth.

Slow-Weathering Grace

Throughout our years in the church, we have been encouraged in song and Scripture to cast our anxieties upon Christ because he cares for us.† Like Mary and Martha, we have sent word to Jesus in prayer, knowing that he loves, he cares, and he can help. We know without a doubt that God will give Jesus whatever he asks.

We kneel by the bed of a loved one or pray at the kitchen table, hours away from the hospital where our friend suffers. Years pass as chronic pain erodes hope. Often with tears, we wait for him to speak and act, reading his word, looking for a shred of assurance. It appears he is silent or sleeping, although we know better. Jesus declared he and his Father are always working.‡

In the same way an iceberg shears from a glacier, God has the capacity to cut away our suffering in an

---

* John 11:44
† 1 Peter 5:7
‡ See John 5:17.

instant. More often, though, he employs a lengthy process more like erosion to accomplish his work.

The gradual work of erosion is as painful to a human heart as it is violent to a natural landscape. Exposure to extreme temperatures and repeated battering by wind and rain shaped the breathtaking landscape of the Badlands of South Dakota into a natural masterpiece. For those who acknowledge God as the director of the wind and water, our hearts turn toward him in awe of what his atmospheric trauma has created.

But in our exposure and battering, we fear he has bobbled the cares we cast. We cannot see the final masterpiece when we are in the middle of his careful "delay." We strain against the wind, rub sand from our eyes, and bemoan his lack of protection. But "God works leisurely because God has eternity to work in."[13] What we see as the end, God calls the middle. He is not wrong, and he is not finished. His loving delays are the process by which he forms us into the image of his Son and shapes us for the praise of his glory.

The challenge for us is to trust his perpetual work when we think he is too slow. When the landscape appears unchanged and the weather wears us down, "we wait in hope for the Lord; he is our help and our shield."* Christ's unhurried work is always the result of his love. When the wait is over and his glory is magnified, we will find our hope has not been denied, only divinely delayed.

~

Dear Lord,

You surprise me with your long processes and drastic measures. I acknowledge I cannot see the end from the beginning as you can. From my view, your delay is cruel. Forgive me for my unbelief.

Remind me that you shape the earth like wax under a seal. Shape me for your glory, I pray. Help me trust your gracious, weathering hand, and teach me to lean on you and not on my own understanding.

Provide patience as I wait to see your glory revealed, whether I must wait hours, days, or until the very "last day." I eagerly anticipate that day when my faith is made sight and my future hope becomes a final reality.

---

* Psalm 33:20

Doubting Hope

Peter Walks on Water

Immediately Jesus made the disciples get into the
boat and go on ahead of him to the other side, while
he dismissed the crowd. After he had dismissed them,
he went up on a mountainside by himself to pray.
Later that night, he was there alone, and the boat was
already a considerable distance from land, buffeted
by the waves because the wind was against it.

Shortly before dawn Jesus went out to them,
walking on the lake. When the disciples saw him
walking on the lake, they were terrified. "It's a
ghost," they said, and cried out in fear.

But Jesus immediately said to them: "Take
courage! It is I. Don't be afraid."

"Lord, if it's you," Peter replied, "tell me to come
to you on the water."

"Come," he said.

Then Peter got down out of the boat, walked on the water and came toward Jesus. But when he saw the wind, he was afraid and, beginning to sink, cried out, "Lord, save me!"

Immediately Jesus reached out his hand and caught him. "You of little faith," he said, "why did you doubt?"

And when they climbed into the boat, the wind died down. Then those who were in the boat worshiped him, saying, "Truly you are the Son of God."

—Matthew 14:22–33

Shoals of fish hid in the long shadow of a boat where the sunset cast its shape upon the water and lengthened it onto the shore. In its evening shade, gulls pecked through sand and reeds searching for snails and shellfish. But an easy meal lay beyond the shadow where two unattended baskets of bread settled in the sand, waiting to be loaded onto the boat. The gulls swooped in for a feast.

Peter ran to the baskets and shooed them away. His brother Andrew was stooped in the boat coiling ropes and rolling sails. "Andrew!" Peter called as he lifted the basket up to the edge. Andrew maneuvered around oars and benches and grabbed the basket. "Put it under the deck to keep the gulls out." Andrew nodded, and Peter lifted the second basket.

It was an enormous amount of bread to keep and store. At home in Capernaum his wife would have a few loaves, but what a laugh she'd get watching him haul baskets of bread instead of fish. *These are only two of twelve,* he'd tell her. She would smack his shoulder with the back of her hand as she had when he'd told her Jesus made wine from water. But when he placed the basket in her mother's lap, they would all be reminded: Jesus, who had healed his mother-in-law's fever in a moment, could also produce bread for thousands in an evening.

The disciples climbed aboard while Jesus remained on the grassy hillside above the beach. He visited with families who were thankful for the food he had multiplied and astonished by the miracle. "Let us stay and help you send them off," Peter had suggested.

"I will join you later," Jesus had said. "I need to be alone with my Father to pray."

"Then please go," Peter urged. "We can dismiss the crowd."

"No," Jesus replied. "You go ahead in the boat to the other side. I will tend to them until they've gone."

With men at their posts, the oars dug against the lake floor, sending swirls of mud to the surface, as Peter shoved out and then swung aboard.

With Peter guiding the steering oar, James, John, Philip, and Andrew tugged at the oars in a synchronized motion that had become as natural and as necessary as walking. Before any of them were strong enough to maneuver a paddle, they'd played in their father's boat, calling pretend orders, casting line and hook, teaming up—two to an oar—to try to put out a bit farther into the water while remaining moored. The fish, they thought, were just beyond the length of their lines.

Bethsaida's shore was the realm where play became work. As their legs stretched long and their arms grew strong, the boys abandoned fishing lines for nets. No longer two to an oar, they sliced through the lake with fluid and measured strokes. But that was on a calm night.

In the dim light of the rising moon, Peter heard the soft crash of waves stirred by breezes barreling down the valleys of Galilee. As he turned to gauge the distance from the shore they'd left at Bethsaida, they collided with the wind.

Above him, the sail was tied, but its loose corners

fluttered and snapped. Peter stood to secure it as a gust tipped the boat to one side. He caught a rope and guided himself hand over hand to the failing knot. He wound it tight, then returned to his post in the stern.

Clouds flew above them, sneaking past the moon. On a clear spring night Peter could identify torches lit on the shores of Bethsaida and the silver reflection from Herod's palace at Tiberius. When neither shore was visible, Orion's starry belt revealed their heading. Tonight, he caught brief glances as he steadied himself long enough to gaze upward.

"Gonna be a long trip!" James hollered over his shoulder from the front.

"Just a headwind," Peter replied. They'd weathered worse.

—

The headwind he had discounted in the early hours of the night now ravaged the lake. Wave upon wave lifted the bow and slammed it into the next breaker. Sailcloth chattered. Crests rose and crashed over the bow, sending currents to the stern, where they pooled and sloshed around Peter's feet.

Words from the Hebrew poet pelted him like mist in the face: "God alone stretches out the heavens and treads on the waves of the sea. He is the Maker of the Bear and Orion, the Pleiades and the constellations of the south. He performs wonders that cannot be fathomed, miracles that cannot be counted."*

Last time the water had been rough, there had been rain and thunder—a terrible storm that threatened to sink them—but on that trip, Jesus had been along. Sleeping, in fact, until Andrew ventured under the bow to beg his help. Peter expected Jesus to bail water, grab the whipping sails, wrangle an oar, or at least shout strengthening words. Instead, he spoke to the wind and waves, and they obeyed him.

But tonight Jesus wasn't onboard. *Tonight it's up to us.* More than half the night was spent. Rowing had deteriorated from synchronized coordination to a slapping chaos. Men groaned as their arms quivered with fatigue. Peter's ankles ached from bracing himself against the bench in front of him. Between his shoulders, muscles burned. Even on his well-calloused hands, blisters bubbled to the surface, then flattened under the friction of wood on skin. What

* Job 9:8–10

should have been the smooth work of an evening had become an all-night struggle.

Peter called orders from the rear to navigate. *Pull. Pull.* The boat dipped into the momentary watery plain, and Peter shouted a cadence. *Row. Row. Row.* The next wave cast itself over the bow and rolled to the back.

"Let's drop the sails and forget fighting this wind!" James hollered. Taut riggings that ran from the mast to the hull vibrated in the wind.

A thought occurred to Peter when he had to pry his fingers off the oar to tighten the sails: *Why are we fighting this? Jesus will not even be in Capernaum when we arrive. If we arrive.* He shoved the thought out of his mind. They could let down the sails, be driven back to shore—any shore—and try again tomorrow in the daylight when the wind died. They'd been battling all night. They had to be close. But when the swells carried the boat upward, Peter saw neither shore.

At the bow, Andrew and Philip were soaked. Peter called the cadence, but their oars skipped across the surface. James had caught a mouthful of lake water and couldn't shake the coughing that had ensued. John's youthful stamina had propelled them through the night, but in these early morning hours, even he had been bested by the relentless wind.

A break in the clouds revealed the moon and lit up the water. Out of the corner of his eye, Peter caught a glimpse of fabric whipping across the waves.

James screamed and began coughing again. He dropped his oar and pointed.

"It's a ghost!" Andrew bellowed.

John had swung from rope to rigging, hiding himself in the stern but peering over the ledge, muttering prayers. His shoulders shook with fatigue and fright.

Peter dropped his oar and clung to the side, shivering and staring at the figure on the lake—a ghost, a phantom—stepping on the surface as if passing by on the shore. It lifted its hands to them, and John screamed.

"Don't be afraid." The voice drifted across the water. "It's me!"

Peter leaned over the pitching edge and sifted through the mist for the familiar face that matched the voice. "Lord!" he shouted over the waves crashing against the boat. "If it's you, tell me to come to you on the water!"

"Come!"

Peter flung himself overboard as waves thrust the boat downward. His feet hit the roiling water. He stepped where he might have swum. Like a toddler on untested legs, he reached for Jesus.

Strands of matted hair whipped and stung Peter's face as he trained his eyes on Jesus. Peter wiped his eyes as Jesus greeted him. Behind them, the mast creaked as it rocked. Unmanned oars banged against the hull. Water weighed down Peter's cloak. Peter glanced around at the wind tossing waves toward him. He whimpered. The surface gave way beneath him, and he sank.

Thrashing to keep himself afloat, he gasped in the frigid deep. *No. Not like this.* Though he heard the men onboard screaming from above, he was disoriented. He searched the darkness for the boat. He meant to scream for a rope, but a wave smacked his head and filled his ear. In the watery silence he shrieked. "Lord! Save me!"

Jesus caught Peter's wrist as he flailed. Clawing at Jesus' arm, Peter was flooded with relief. Jesus lifted him out and set his feet upon the water. "You of little faith," Jesus said. "Why did you doubt me?"

Peter had no answer.

The men on the boat swayed with the wind but held fast to the ropes, like seaweed caught in a net. With Jesus at his elbow, Peter flung his arms over the boat's edge, his mind rocking between panic and awe. Andrew and Philip grabbed him by the shoulders and dragged him onto the deck.

John and James steadied Jesus as he climbed in and the wind died.

Loosened sailcloth swished against itself. Oars barely rattled in their rings as the lake became a glassy plain. James coughed again. Jesus wrung out his sleeves. Peter's head ached as lake water drained from his nose. He flopped to his knees on the deck, exhausted. How foolish he had been to believe it was up to him to navigate alone. What a relief to hear the voice of Jesus. Why did he think that he who treads on water would set him there to drown? King David's song rang in his heart: "The LORD protects the unwary; when I was brought low, he saved me. Return to your rest, my soul, for the LORD has been good to you."*

Gulls squawked overhead. Peter heard the soft hiss of a cast net splashing on the lake. The boat lurched, and everyone staggered toward the front. With no one tending the steering oar, it had lodged in the shallow

---

* Psalm 116:6–7

floor of a harbor. They had arrived. When or how, Peter couldn't explain. But as sure as the lavender horizon announced the morning, they were at the shore. He bowed his head and breathed a declaration. "You are truly the Son of God."

Peter's Pendulum

It was a declaration he made more than once, and it was the confession on which Christ Jesus promised to build his church. Peter's conviction propelled him to regular and hasty acts of devotion that often ended badly... at first.

Peter's hope in Christ was something of a pendulum swinging between the heights of devotion and the lows of cowardice, between the crests of belief and hope and the depths of doubt. In every instance Jesus stood opposite of Peter with a hand extended to bring him down from zeal or to draw him from his shame.

It was the pattern of Peter's *years* as a disciple. He believed without a doubt Jesus was "the Christ of God." But he believed in the Messiah his nation expected—a triumphant ruler rather than a slain sacrifice.

It wasn't an unfounded view. Right after Peter made his great confession that Jesus was the Christ of God, Jesus blessed Peter and told him he'd build a church on that truth and the gates of hell would not keep it from advancing. Later, he promised to give him the "keys of the kingdom of heaven!"* On another occasion Jesus comforted his disciples with apparent visions of grandeur: "At the renewal of all things, when the Son of Man sits on his glorious throne, you who have followed me will also sit on twelve thrones, judging the twelve tribes of Israel."†

When Jesus first predicted his suffering and death, Peter was compelled to take Jesus aside and "correct" him. "Never, Lord! This shall never happen to you!"‡ But perhaps underneath the courage was a current of fright. If the king suffers and dies, what becomes of those who've been slated to rule with him?

Jesus plucked him from the heights of self-reliant loyalty with a rebuke of his own. "Get behind me, Satan!...You do not have in mind the concerns of

---

* Matthew 16:19
† Matthew 19:28
‡ Matthew 16:22

God, but merely human concerns."* It sounded harsh, but it was the quickest way to help Peter out of his wrong expectations. Peter felt the waves tumbling in around him. He thought he was devoted to Jesus, but Jesus showed Peter that he was devoted to his own expectation of what Jesus ought to do.

Otherworldly Kingdom

Peter *was* destined for leadership in Christ's kingdom, but his kingdom was "not of this world."† The greatness and influence Peter hoped for came through means he did not expect or desire. Training for ruling in Christ's otherworldly kingdom meant taking up a cross instead of a scepter. Preparation to serve the King meant stooping low to cleanse the filthy feet of brothers and betrayers alike.

But Peter did not understand. In the final chapters of Jesus' time on earth, Peter finds himself at odds with the Christ of God whom he'd been so determined to serve.

---

* Matthew 16:23
† John 18:36

"I am among you as one who serves, and I will wash your feet."

"You shall never wash my feet."*

"One of you will betray me."

"Surely you don't mean me?"†

"You will all fall away."

"Even if all fall away, I will not."‡

"This very night, before the rooster crows, you will disown me three times."

"Even if I have to die with you, I will never disown you."§

As the night of the Last Supper wore on, Peter's expectations splashed into foam and evaporated. Dedication churned into panic. At Jesus' arrest, Peter raised the sword of devotion, swung for the head of the high priest's servant, but only caught his ear. Jesus

---

* Luke 22:27 and John 13:7–8
† Mark 14:18–19
‡ Mark 14:27–29
§ Matthew 26:34–35

condemned Peter's valiant resolve as untimely and unnecessary. He healed the servant on the spot.*

In the space of a few hours Peter plummeted from sword-swinging valor to cursing and terrified denial. Stripped of his devotion to the kind of king he expected, Peter proved himself unworthy and unqualified for the kind of leadership he wanted.

Peter found himself sinking not in the waves of the Sea of Galilee but in waves of despair. He went out and wept bitterly.† All was lost. Dead kings don't rule, and disloyal cowards don't deserve respect.

Peter was eager for heroics, but he was not prepared for the humiliation of grace—receiving the undeserved favor of the One he denied.

On the morning shores of the Sea of Galilee, Jesus lifted Peter once again from the suffocating waves of regret and restored him to the position he'd called him to all along—greatness that comes from having been sifted. With the chaff of self-reliance and self-determination blown away, the transformed leader is equipped with humility. His tasks will be less like barking orders and more like feeding and shepherding

---

* See Luke 22:50–51.
† Luke 22:62

God's flock. He will no longer glare around the table ready to pounce upon traitors. Instead, he'll strengthen his brothers, knowing he is capable of the worst and the recipient of the best.

Peter would one day pen strengthening words to encourage the flock Christ commissioned him to serve.

> Praise be to the God and Father of our Lord Jesus Christ! In his great mercy he has given us new birth into a living hope through the resurrection of Jesus Christ from the dead, and into an inheritance that can never perish, spoil or fade. This inheritance is kept in heaven for you, who through faith are shielded by God's power until the coming of the salvation that is ready to be revealed in the last time. In all this you greatly rejoice, though now for a little while you may have had to suffer grief in all kinds of trials. These have come so that the proven genuineness of your faith—of greater worth than gold, which perishes even though refined by fire— may result in praise, glory and honor when Jesus Christ is revealed.*

---

* 1 Peter 1:3–7

Peter received what Christ had promised, and though it was not what Peter expected, it was more than he'd ever imagined.

Disciples Refined, Hope Revived

Peter has been labeled as a man who acted without thinking. Some have called him the disciple with the foot-shaped mouth. To a degree those descriptions fit, but to start or stop there is to miss the beauty of what Jesus did with his quick-speaking, impulsive disciple. If, in our mind's eye, we stand above Peter tsk-tsking him for being impetuous, we squander an opportunity to worship God for the way he revives and redeems.

Before Peter was rock-solid, before he was strengthening his brothers, he was swinging swords and making impossible declarations as a staunch defender of the future King of Israel. In his exuberance Peter didn't have the whole picture of what Jesus came to do, and *Jesus chose Peter anyway.*

That comes as a great comfort to those of us cut from the same cloth. While we were still confused about who Jesus was and what he came to do, he chose us!

Jesus loved Peter too much to leave him in

ignorance. The whipping wind and the darkness of despair led Peter to long for Jesus. Although it can be frightening and uncomfortable, Jesus does the same for us. To fulfill our commission in his kingdom, we must be plucked from the delusions of misunderstanding, so that we will set our hope fully—and only—on Christ.

Mistaken Expectations

We are sometimes prone to mistake our expectations for Christ's promises. With enthusiasm we place our hope in Christ and expect him to repay us with favors of comfortable relationships, material blessings, and financial rewards. But when we find ourselves suffocating in the pounding waves of disappointed people, deteriorating possessions, or devastated finances, we become frightened. The terrifying circumstances mock us: "You hoped in vain!"

As we cry to Jesus for rescue, he teaches us that he is our comfort, not because he stills all storms but because he walks with us on the turbulent sea of life. His hand of provision shows that his primary blessing is the gift of peace, because he has proven trustworthy. Christ Jesus demonstrates that he is our great reward as he rescues us from mistaken expectations. He establishes our feet upon the solid hope that is "Christ in you, the hope of glory."*

———

Dear Lord,

Thank you for choosing wobbly, impulsive people like me.

I confess that when waves of hardship and uncertainty rage around me, I waffle between defending and defecting.

Teach me, Lord, to keep my hope fixed on you when failure stings. Prompt me to call on you for rescue when I'm sinking in doubt. Lift me from self-reliance to the firm shore of dependence on you.

May the waves of adversity wash away my expectations that are out of line with yours. May my heart be anchored because I hope in you.

---

* Colossians 1:27.

Unimaginable Hope

Mary the Mother of Jesus

Near the cross of Jesus stood his mother, his mother's sister, Mary the wife of Clopas, and Mary Magdalene. When Jesus saw his mother there, and the disciple whom he loved standing nearby, he said to her, "Woman, here is your son," and to the disciple, "Here is your mother." From that time on, this disciple took her into his home.

Later, knowing that everything had now been finished, and so that Scripture would be fulfilled, Jesus said, "I am thirsty." A jar of wine vinegar was there, so they soaked a sponge in it, put the sponge on a stalk of the hyssop plant, and lifted it to Jesus' lips. When he had received the drink, Jesus said, "It is finished."

With that, he bowed his head and gave up his spirit.

—John 19:25–30
Parallel Passages: Mark 15:36–40, Matthew
27:48–55

A pair of cavernous voids in the hillside resembled the empty sockets of an enormous skull—the namesake of this place for executions. The air was thick with the odor of Roman leather steeped in the sweat of battle. Morning dampness lingered and carried the stench of blood and urine, vinegar and wine. The sun refused to burn it off, and fitting nausea rumbled inside Mary. How could she gaze upon this travesty without feelings of sickness?

Through tears she read the sign fixed above her son's head. The executioner had shouted the charges along the road as they'd exited the city: "Jesus of Nazareth, King of the Jews." In the span of a week his kinsmen had hailed him as their saving king and then the leaders had conspired to kill him.

Mary had known God to speak through angels, dreams, the prophecies of elderly saints, and Jesus himself. But this morning, angels were absent. No visions appeared during her restless night. Elderly saints had passed long ago.

Jesus struggled for breath and prayed intermittently. His eyes flitted closed, then opened at the startling jeers from the crowd. His head was misshapen with purple lumps where he'd been struck. Swelling forced open split skin, and flies buzzed at the edges of the cut. Cheeks she'd kissed were streaked with blood. Hair she'd combed and trimmed was tangled with thorns. Fingers that had once curled around hers were paralyzed and splayed by iron spikes.

"Oh God!" she prayed. "You said he would be great. You said he would reign on David's throne forever. He is your Son! No word from you can fail, but I tremble at the thwarting of all you've promised."

If God had spoken today, Mary hadn't heard him. Roman swords clattered in their sheaths as soldiers wove between three crosses. Their gruesome work of execution was nothing more than a dirty chore likely to last for days.

A centurion barked orders. "Raise the gall!" A soldier jabbed a sponge on the end of a hyssop reed, dipped it into a jar, and thrust it toward Jesus' mouth. Jesus flinched and turned his head.

They laughed. "Not the kind you like, eh?"

"Nah!" called another. "He's used to fine wine!" Hoisting his spear into the air, he tapped the sign affixed over Jesus' head. He smacked the spearhead under each word and spat, "King of the Jews." His face twisted in feigned surprise at seeing a king on a cross. "Only fine wine for him!"

Mary felt herself crumbling. *Fine wine.* Her mind rushed back to Cana, embarrassed by the anticipation she had felt that day. Jesus had entered the wedding hall followed by a small group of disciples calling him "Rabbi." Her heart was brimming with hope. All those years she had known he was the Messiah. But it was a truth she'd cradled, like a babe snuggled close to his mother's chest until he could walk alone. Mary observed his followers imitating Jesus, emulating his greetings, insisting Jesus take the honored seat at the table. The cherished truth finally wriggled from her chest, and she sang a familiar refrain: "My soul glorifies the Lord and my spirit rejoices in God my Savior."*

Such a lovely occasion. I'm so glad he brought his disciples. God is fulfilling his word. Jesus—my Jesus—will sit on David's throne forever! He will save us. She smiled and marveled. Indeed, she was blessed and

---

* Luke 1:46–47

favored, and it still left her speechless with wonder and thanksgiving.

Boughs of flowering myrtle wound around pillars surrounding the dining room. From where Mary stood, Jesus appeared to be seated between two that had a garland of ivy draped between them, as if the greenery insisted he be enthroned. She was delighting herself with visions of his regal future when someone grabbed her arm. Mary turned to see her sister, Salome, pale and biting her thumb. Her eyes darted around the room as though she'd misplaced something.

"Mary." Her voice quivered, and she mumbled around her thumb. "I don't know how... I'm sure there were... it was planned... but I thought there were..." she stammered.

"What? What happened?"

"We've run out of wine!" Tears pooled in her eyes. "Oh Mary! We've disgraced our son... at his wedding feast!" She pressed trembling fingers to her lips to hush the humiliating news.

Mary didn't know what to say. Wine was an expected luxury at this celebration. Guests would come and go for the rest of the week, and the shortage would mark their family as inhospitable, careless, or at best, impoverished. Where could they buy enough wine to last through the next days of this wedding-feast week when it had taken a year to plan for what had already run out? More important, what would they serve at the next meal?

Musicians plucked strings and trilled their flutes. Festive tunes muffled whispers of an impending disgrace the musicians knew nothing about. Little girls with mouths full of almonds and fists full of flower petals danced in the aisles. Salome dodged them and bustled toward her husband in a panic.

Mary wove between the tables, placing her hand on the head of a twirling little girl as she squeezed by her. Mary stepped around the feet of reclining guests, peering into wine jars as she passed each one. *Empty. Gone.* A red ring circled each jar's base.

Jesus visited with his followers as they reclined on pillows around the low table. Where he pointed, they focused their attention. When he spoke, they leaned in. One lifted an empty glass to his lips and, realizing it was empty, set it back down.

Mary strode toward Jesus, knelt beside him, and laid a hand on his shoulder to steady herself. He smiled. She spoke quietly. "They have no more wine."

A young man at the table reached for the wine jar and tipped it to look inside. "Ours is gone," he said.

"Dear woman, why does that involve me? My time has not yet come."

Mary stood. Jesus prioritized his Father's work, in his Father's time, and, as a young boy, in his Father's house. Now, as a grown man beginning a public ministry, he would still defer to his Father's timing. The glory of his Father was at the forefront of his mind. One day, that glory would be proclaimed at the coronation of her Son as Israel's true and long-awaited king.

Two servants rushed to their table, bringing more food and water to distract from the lack of wine. One set a plate full of sliced bread in front of Jesus at the head of the table, and Mary caught his arm. "Do whatever he tells you," she said as she nodded toward Jesus. She hurried away to comfort Salome.

Bread dwindled to crumbs, cheese curled at the edges, hollowed pomegranate shells wobbled on plates. Six enormous stone water jars lined the back wall of the wedding hall. Servants lined up like ants marching past the jars, refilling each stone vessel one pitcher at a time, returning again and again until they had all been filled.

Mary sat with her sister as Salome reported, "We have sent word to the vineyards for any available wine to be brought at once, but no one has come."

"Look, Salome, our cousins from Judea are enjoying themselves." Mary tried to ease her mind. The group had traveled all day to attend the celebration. Their table was strewn with bones, gristle, apple cores, and naked grape stems. Peals of laughter thundered, and four empty wine jars sat at the end of the table waiting to be cleared. No one had complained. No one had noticed. Yet.

The head waiter motioned to Salome's son and called him away from his bride. He chuckled and slapped the bridegroom on the back. "You served your cheap wine first and are just now giving us the fine wine!" He laughed. Salome blinked. Her husband peered into the man's glass.

At the back of the hall, two servants hovered around the water jars, smiling and staring down at their blushing reflections. Mary's heart pounded. Perhaps his hour had come. *My Jesus. Israel's Messiah.* He had saved their honor.

"He saved others! But he can't save himself!" The scoffing jolted Mary from past visions of hope. Religious leaders from the temple joined the mocking. They boasted of a righteousness that no one could mimic, but they lobbed insults that would make good men cringe. Their wicked dance brought them close to the crosses so their disdain would be felt and sent them reeling backward so they wouldn't be spattered with blood. "If you could get down from that cross, O king of Israel, then we would believe you!"

"Kings need a pointy crown," said the centurion on duty, gesturing to the thorns pressed around Jesus' head. "And fine garments like this one!" Jesus had been stripped, and his few garments lay in a soiled pile. The centurion held up the full-length garment, wrapped the sleeves around his neck, and let it flap in the breeze behind him, as though it were a royal cape. "My robe!" he declared.

Salome gasped. "Oh Mary! It's the one we made." Mary nodded and shushed her.

Another soldier snatched it from his neck. "Why do you get it?" He twirled it around examining the quality. "Look at this, it's woven into one piece. No seams."

"It's not yours!" The first grabbed it back. "Let's roll dice for it. First to get doubles wins." Stooped below her dying son, they played their games.

God! What will you do? What are you doing? Have mercy on your Son. Have mercy on us! Horses stamped around the execution grounds, throwing their manes from side to side and laying piles of dung wherever they pleased. Tack rattled as their riders drove them back and forth in front of the crosses to keep mourners away.

Groans erupted, and the lucky soldier waved the woven garment above his head like a flag. The loser sucked a wineskin dry. The blood-red plume on his helmet wobbled as he stumbled and cursed his luck. Another ripped a barley loaf with his teeth. His leather boot sank in the bloodied mud where he stood.

Mary leaned against her sister. The women who had followed Jesus through Galilee were there too, lending support and tears. Like kindling sticks, they trembled together over the fire of grief. Her son, falsely convicted, crucified, and deposed from kingship before he'd been enthroned. His court of disciples was nowhere to be found.

"Salome," Mary cried, "where are his disciples when he suffers?"

Salome ran her hand across Mary's shoulders. "John is here." Salome discreetly waved at him to come. John joined the small group of women but offered no comfort except his presence.

"How can this be?" Mary cried. No one answered.

"He will save his people from their sins," the angel had declared to Joseph, and Joseph had encouraged her with the same words over the years. *How can it be, God? How can he save his people when they are the ones who convicted him?*

"A sword will pierce your own soul too," Simeon had warned. In three decades she had not forgotten. Reminders pricked her soul. Neighbors had labeled him an illegitimate son. Heart-wrenching panic had twisted that sword as she and Joseph had ransacked Jerusalem looking for Jesus only to find him in his Father's temple. When he disappeared for months of ministry, when jealous rumors trundled down from Jerusalem, when religious leaders called him a devil, she'd felt the bloodletting of her heart and soul.

Today, the sword Simeon had foretold had run all the way through. As she ached for him, bewildered by the cruel end of his Father's work, she knew she would do it all again to have the privilege of loving him and being loved by him.

He opened his eyes and said, "Dear woman, here is your son." His head fell toward John. Then, staring at John, he said, "Here is your mother."

John stepped between the women and came to Mary's side. "I will take care of you, Mary." *Oh God, even as he dies, he is a perfect son. Do you grieve with me?*

The sun was high, and shadows were short. Mary

listened for God's comfort, but he answered with darkness that snuffed out the midday brightness.

A horse spooked and bolted. His hooves thundered down the hillside, and his rider screamed for him to stop. Soldiers cursed and called for torches. Salome clung to Mary, and Mary clung to John. The other women pressed in as if huddling would keep them from being trampled.

Darkness hovered for hours. Soldiers subdued by the untimely nightfall sat around a fire for light and warmth. Reduced to the realization that Rome's military strength could not command the daylight, the place of the skull quieted. Disoriented birds returned to treetops. Insects abandoned their feast of flesh and blood and swarmed the flames instead.

Mary shivered as she prayed, "Oh God, what are you doing? Is your love declared in the grave? Are your wonders known in the place of darkness? You have taken my loved one from me; darkness is my closest friend."* Though God had not sent an angel, though his voice had not thundered, he had spread his grief across the sky.

"My God!" Jesus cried. "Why have you forsaken

---

* See Psalm 88.

me?" His voice was tired and dry. "I thirst..." A soldier ran for the sponge and lifted it to his lips. This time he drank. Inside her chest, Mary felt as if something had ripped open. Breath was scarce.

With shaking legs, Jesus pushed against the spike driven through his feet. He pulled against the nails piercing his hands and struggled to lift his chest and fill his lungs. As he exhaled, he cried, "It is finished!"

Mary heard an unearthly groan and realized it was her own voice. Sobs wracked her shoulders. She folded. Salome laced her arm through Mary's to keep her upright. John spoke, but Mary couldn't make out his words. Rumbling filled the air. Rocks rattled from the hillside. A centurion croaked for order as another screamed for Neptune to stop shaking the earth.

Mary's legs threatened to crumple underneath her. All around, women cried. With her eyes shut, Mary felt as if she were spinning.

The earth stilled.

"Mary!" John's rough hands pressed against her cheeks. "Mary! Look at me." Mary opened her eyes. "Mary, we should go..."

Mary turned one last time, searching the darkness for glimmers of hope. By the light of a few torches, she saw his body sag from a swaying cross.

—

Mary sat up, panting. Roman soldiers and chief priests had chased her into her dreams with whips and spears as she'd stumbled through Jerusalem alone, crying out to God.

In answer, he had whisked her to wakefulness and reminded her of the safety of John's house. Mary hardly remembered arriving. John had urged her to eat, but the thought of food had made her gag, and she'd collapsed on this mat.

The Sabbath had been a blur. John's house quivered with fright. Peter had arrived sometime that day looking a mess. Mary didn't have the will to ask where he'd been. Others trickled in throughout the day, quiet and ashamed, skittish and anxious, but confined to the house by Sabbath laws and outright fear.

Predawn light cast a window-shaped beam on the opposite wall. She must have slept. The nightmares were proof. But Mary was exhausted. Dreams of threads of skin hanging from Jesus' back had made her want to run to him, but soldiers with teeth of broken pottery had beaten her back. Between nightmares she had cried in prayer. "O God! You brought your Son without the help of a husband. Will you bring salvation for Israel without your Son?" She curled into the blankets and sobbed, "I do not understand. You can thwart the plans of nations, and the purposes of people, but your plans stand firm... don't they?"* She sifted through Scripture in her heart for refuge and comfort, but each time she ended with questions. "You will not grant the desires of the wicked... but haven't you, Lord?"†

In the night Salome had brought her water. Mary took a sip, set the cup by her bed, and lay down again. She drifted off, wishing to dream of the days when Jesus had played with his brothers and held their hands as they'd walked to synagogue. As she sank into sweet rest, the front door slammed open.

Scrambling from her mat, she threw on her cloak, straining to sort out the commotion in the next room. *Romans? Religious leaders?* She covered her mouth to silence her breathing, but her heart pounded in her aching head. She pressed her other hand against her temple to ease the pain and felt the throbbing in her fingertips. Women chattered, high and excited. John shushed them, but they did not heed him. Mary

---

* See Psalm 33:10–11.
† See Psalm 140:8.

backed herself into a corner to catch her breath, to wait for the headache to wane, and to listen.

"Tomb was open…light inside…men with dazzling white robes." Mary had seen that kind of dazzling robe, flashing with light. God had not sent an angel to the cross, but he had sent one to the tomb. She flew from her room as Salome exclaimed, "He has risen!"

Mary had no doubt.

A Mother Convinced

The last time Mary, the mother of Jesus, is mentioned in the Gospels, we find her at the foot of the cross— a firsthand witness to the finished work of Christ. She knew her trustworthy God had fulfilled his word to her and to Israel in unexplainable and unexpected ways over the years. But she could neither understand nor explain his crucifixion.

When Gabriel appeared to a young and unjaded Mary, he proclaimed she would carry God's Son. Based on Scriptures and teaching she'd heard at synagogue, she believed God would send his Son to be his servant on earth, to be the rightful and righteous ruler of Israel, and to save his people. As the angel described the child she would bear, she knew he was talking about the Messiah. Her perplexity was not about who was coming or why but about how a virgin could bear a child. When he explained the supernatural "how," Mary believed.

No one knew better than Mary that Jesus was God's son. At his conception, the Holy Spirit overshadowed her. At Jesus' birth, God provided the privacy of a stable, the witnesses of shepherds, and the testimony of angels. When the decree of genocide thundered from Jerusalem, God carried his Son and his earthly parents off to Egypt. When it was safe to return, he planted the little family in the obscurity of Nazareth.

In three decades, God moved her from Nazareth, to Bethlehem, to Egypt, back to Nazareth, to Capernaum, and to Jerusalem. She was a busy mother of at least seven children.* Joseph's absence from much of the New Testament leads scholars to believe she was a widowed single mother for at least part of her children's growing-up years.

Mary was no stranger to upheaval, accusation,

---

* Matthew 13:55–56

grief, and loss. Religious leaders in Jerusalem called Jesus a devil, and his brothers said he was "out of his mind."* The Jewish population at large called him Elijah or John the Baptist come back to life. For a while, his disciples called him a prophet, then teacher, and when he proved himself to be much more, they asked one another, "Who is this?"†

Throughout Mary's life the unbelievers clamored, "Convince us he is the Son of God!" Too much had transpired for Mary to doubt the angel's declaration that Jesus would be called the Son of God.‡ With a mental scroll full of God's demonstrated faithfulness, Mary answered, "You'll have to convince me that he's not."

When they killed him, dark doubt must have strained at the dual bonds of divine and familial love. The spiritual upheaval caused by an earthquake of killed hope must have shaken the obedient handmaiden of God. The one who had pledged allegiance to God by saying, "I am the Lord's servant"§ found herself spiritually and emotionally devastated.

---

* Mark 3:21
† Mark 4:41
‡ See Luke 1:35.
§ Luke 1:38 (NIV, 1984)

What Mary Didn't Know Still Hurt Her

Jesus had explained his coming suffering. He'd warned his disciples that he would be betrayed, mocked, spat upon, flogged, killed, and raised on the third day.* But even with the warning and the promise of resurrection, the disciples fled and scattered.

It doesn't appear that Mary was privy to such teaching. If she had heard about it, the news came from disciples who couldn't explain what they didn't understand. No matter how many times Jesus told them, they remained mystified. "It was hidden from them, so that they did not grasp it, and they were afraid to ask him about it."†

What Mary Knew Sustained Her

Imagine the wrestling of hope and doubt, faith and fear, trust and uncertainty that must have plagued Mary. What terrible questions did she ask herself about her role as mother? What questions did she ask of God?

---

* See Luke 18:32–33.
† Luke 9:45

Did she have any inkling of the eternal, spiritual work Jesus accomplished while she watched him be brutally killed before her eyes? Was she surprised by the first whispers of his resurrection? Or did she hear it with a striking familiarity of expecting the unexpected?

God had assured Mary that Jesus would be great. He would rule forever, and his kingdom would never end. Mary never questioned whether God meant what he said. As Jesus grew, Mary did not dispute his calling. She believed, and Luke tells us she "treasured up all these things and pondered them in her heart."* At the crucifixion, she must have wondered, "How can a dead Messiah rule forever?" And perhaps God whispered in her heart, once again, the assurance that "nothing is impossible with God."†

Your Sorrow Will Turn to Joy

The last time Mary is mentioned in the Bible, we find her in a large upstairs room somewhere in Jerusalem among 120 believers. Seven weeks had passed since

---

* Luke 2:19
† Luke 1:37 (NIV, 1984)

Jesus had been killed and raised. The eleven scattered disciples were regathered. His unbelieving brothers were now counted among the believers. "The women" who discovered the empty tomb were present. Together they were *all* praying constantly and waiting for God to send the promised gift of his Holy Spirit.*

When a sound like violent wind and something akin to tongues of fire rested upon those 120 believers, Mary must have sensed a holy familiarity. Perhaps in her mind she was whisked back to her childhood home in Nazareth, where, as a young lady, the Holy Spirit had come upon her to set his redemptive work in motion. Thirty years later God, who had formed a baby in the virgin's womb, withdrew the foretold sword of suffering from her soul and replaced it with his Holy Spirit! Her son and her Savior continually present and living in her—the guarantee of hope fulfilled.

Hope for Impossibilities

Two millennia later, with the gift of God's written word, the presence of His Spirit in our lives, and the

---

* See Acts 1:14–15.

testimony of believers before us, we still wobble on the edge of hopeless unbelief, as if a few things are impossible, even for God.

Our lives are marred by evidence of hopeless situations. We drag loved ones from the pit of addiction only to hear they've crawled back to the pleasures of self-destruction. Children wage wars of calculated rebellion against parents who have tried hard to love them. Choices they have been warned about entice them precisely because of the warnings they've received. Illnesses ravage body and mind. The flames of newlywed marital bliss are doused by everything from fatigue to boredom to violation of vows. We are no strangers to upheaval and impossibility.

Like Mary, we hurt as we witness the excruciating death of dreams, expectations, or loved ones. God does not always prevent the casualties. We stumble from the ruins carrying remnants and mementos of what we expected God to do.

"Hope that is seen is no hope at all," says the apostle Paul. "Who hopes for what they already have? But if we hope for what we do not yet have, we wait for it patiently."* It's in the waiting, when we can't imagine

---

* Romans 8:24–25 (NLT)

how God could accomplish his plan, that we must trust his timing and infinite wisdom.

"The wisdom we speak of is the mystery of God—his plan that was previously hidden, even though he made it for our ultimate glory before the world began. But the rulers of this world have not understood it; if they had, they would not have crucified our glorious Lord. That is what the Scriptures mean when they say,

> *'No eye has seen, no ear has heard,*
> *and no mind has imagined*
> *what God has prepared*
> *for those who love him.'"**

The Roman and Jewish rulers did not understand, so they crucified Jesus. The disciples did not understand, so they fled. The women did not understand, so they brought spices for his burial. But God is not limited by our understanding, and he is not confined to what we can conceive.

Hope based on Christ is an invisible future certainty. Like Mary, we cling to his word. It remains

---

* 2 Corinthians 2:7–9 (NLT)

true even if our experience says otherwise and the outcome is unimaginable, because nothing is impossible with God.

—

Dear Lord,

I have tried to imagine how you might bring good from what appears to be a disaster, and it seems impossible.

I know your ways are not like mine and your thoughts are higher. I confess I cannot conceive of what you have prepared for me on earth or in heaven. I am prone to squander peace of mind by conjuring solutions that discount your power.

Teach me to wait with hope and confidence that you will accomplish exactly what you meant. Help me trust your perfect timeline when it seems I've messed it up.

May I live with assurance that one day the invisible and internal good you complete in me will be revealed as a masterpiece that glorifies your artistry.

Do your unimaginable work in me, I pray.

Confused Hope

Two Disciples on the Emmaus Road

Now that same day two of them were going to a village called Emmaus, about seven miles from Jerusalem. They were talking with each other about everything that had happened. As they talked and discussed these things with each other, Jesus himself came up and walked along with them; but they were kept from recognizing him.

He asked them, "What are you discussing together as you walk along?"

They stood still, their faces downcast. One of them, named Cleopas, asked him, "Are you the only one visiting Jerusalem who does not know the things that have happened there in these days?"

"What things?" he asked.

"About Jesus of Nazareth," they replied. "He was a prophet, powerful in word and deed before God and all the people. The chief priests and our rulers handed him over to be sentenced to death, and they crucified him; but we had hoped that he was the one who was going to redeem Israel. And what is more, it is the third day since all this took place."

—Luke 24:13–21

Parallel Passage: Mark 16:12–13

On the eve of the Sabbath a dwindling band of Jesus' followers had limped back to John's house, sheltered by eerie afternoon darkness. They had arrived a few at a time, wounded by shards of shattered hope and haunted by beatings and blood. John had supported Jesus' grieving mother as they staggered through the door in time for the beginning of the Sabbath—a day to rest.

But for Cleopas, there had been no rest at all. Hiding indoors and whispering Passover songs reminded him they were now the hunted ones. Like fish trapped in a pool after tides roll out to sea, they were stuck, ready to dart at the slightest ripple.

Pounding on the gate sent everyone scurrying about the room, ready to resist or flee the commotion outside.

"John! Let us in!" Mary's voice accompanied the pounding.

As John opened the door, the faint aroma of myrrh and spice rushed in with the breeze.

Mary and the women huddling around her stumbled in. "Someone has opened the tomb! Jesus is not there." The little jar of burial fragrance shook in her trembling hands. "We were there…and we saw angels! He has risen from the dead!"

Cleopas blinked into the sun-gilded window. Had they been drowning their grief with strong drinks? Nonsense punctuated by great gasps tumbled from their lips.

Peter pushed by them. John rushed outside, and the women trailed him. An ornate pot filled with burial spices sat next to Mary's little jar on the table, forgotten.

Their carelessness agitated Cleopas. Trouble simmered in Jerusalem. If the cauldron was bumped by this idle tale that sent half their number into the street—to the tomb no less—Cleopas feared they would reveal themselves as grieving fools or, worse, suffer the same fate as Jesus.

As Peter, John, and the women rushed to the tomb, Cleopas and his friend Isaac fled from Jerusalem.

They scuttled through alleys, distancing themselves from the hasty disciples wandering through burial grounds.[14] The sun had risen, but houses still provided cover as they fled from shadow to shadow.

Swift and heavy, something swooped overhead. It dove into the alley before them and snatched a mouse. Cleopas pressed a hand to his chest. Isaac leaned against a wall, his face chalky. Ascending on silver wings, an owl screeched good day to Jerusalem as the sun chased him into the trees.

Cleopas swallowed. "It's fine. It's nothing." He said it for himself as much as for Isaac. He grabbed Isaac's sleeve. "This way." Together they hustled toward a western gate leading out of the city. Roman guards would be stationed there, he was sure of that. But with Passover behind them and trade resuming this morning, he planned to shuffle past them under the guise of normal routine.

Although this week had been anything but routine. Cleopas and Isaac had arrived in Jerusalem ahead of Jesus in time for the grand spectacle of his welcome. With the raving crowd shouting "Hosanna!" Cleopas had thrown his cloak into the road on the outside chance that Israel's future king might do him the favor of trampling it. Palm branches strewn among the garments had formed a patchwork of temporary carpet for an eternal ruler.

Then, like the flick of a horsemen's whip, the celebration had careened into a nightmare as their own rulers had enlisted the Romans to execute their friend and Messiah.

Cleopas hung his head. Toward the hem of his cloak, the stain of a squashed palm frond bounced against his leg as he walked.

As he and Isaac approached the yawning archway of the city gate, rumors swarmed like locusts.

His disciples defected.

One hanged.

His body stolen.

Nothing but a hoax.

Lazarus being stalked.

Sheep rustled through the arch toward the temple, following their shepherd. A woman hugged a basket of eggs against her hip as she dodged them. Behind her, a cart loaded with rounds of cheese rattled toward the market, its driver hunched and hidden behind its bounty. As their countrymen funneled in, the two men slipped out. Cleopas didn't dare mention it here, but talk of a scandal scared him.

He glanced backward as the road sloped gently

away from the city and hurried the two men toward home. Rome had built this road with slabs, strength, and carefully fitted paving stones. Although it was well traveled, stubborn grass pushed sunward through the cracks. Cleopas kept his eyes down, tracing the green sprigs and recalling Isaiah's words: "Surely the people are grass. The grass withers and the flowers fall, but the word of our God endures forever."*

Meals on hillsides, nights in the desert, blistered feet and aching legs had been no burden when Jesus was their living hope. His kingdom talk strengthened their resolve, and Cleopas had felt certain Jesus was the promise of God's enduring word. But now, hopes of a king and kingdom, a righteous priest, and a wise prophet were as withered and fallen as the man they had followed.

Some distance from the city, the road leveled toward the valley. Blossoming almond branches bent over the road and cried their last few petals. Jerusalem shrank in the distance behind them. By midday, travelers had thinned out. Without an incline hurrying them from Jerusalem, and with the cool air swimming in the valley, their pace slowed.

---

* Isaiah 40:7–8

In the absence of fellow travelers, Isaac finally spoke. "Who could have dreamed Passover would end like this?"

"Who could have dreamed it would have started as it did?" Cleopas shook his head. With shock and rebellious glee, they had watched as Jesus had upended tables in the temple. Coins had rolled and clattered as money changers scrambled to retrieve them. Doves had escaped the open court. "I was convinced he was the Messiah."

"We all were," Isaac reminded him.

"Your father is going to scold us when we get home," Cleopas lamented.

"He scolded us when we left. I dishonored him when I followed a false messiah."

"But none of the rebels who came before him did what Jesus did," Cleopas argued. "How else can we explain a lifelong cripple dancing in the temple? Or blind men giving directions by landmarks? He was different."

"I know. But like those who came before, he died. The prophets say the Messiah will carry the weight of government on his shoulders and his peace will last forever."

Cleopas threw his hands in the air. "How can

any king rule forever? Look at Herod. Under Rome, Herod is fragile."

"Right, and Jesus didn't even depose him! Herod still reigns, and the Romans still oppress. The rest of us are bereaved of our friend and seen as fools!"

Footsteps behind them hushed Cleopas' response. He bristled at being called a fool. Volatile times required careful steps, and he held his tongue.

Cleopas grabbed the end of a willow tree that brushed his arm. He squeezed the branch and stripped its silver leaves as he slowed to let the stranger pass. Cleopas pointed to nothing at the base of the tree and feigned interest. Isaac stumbled to a stop but didn't take the cue. He muttered, "What? I don't see anything."

Instead of passing, the stranger sidled up to Isaac. "What are you two discussing?"

Cleopas let the handful of leaves twirl to the ground, calculating the man's interest.

"I could see your dispute from back there." He threw a thumb over his shoulder.

Dread rumbled in Cleopas' stomach. *Foolish and careless!* Not wanting to divulge his former allegiances, he answered cautiously, "Are you visiting Jerusalem? Haven't you heard about the things that happened in the past few days?"

"What things?"

Like the reckless fool his father had called him, Isaac plunged in. "About Jesus of Nazareth!"

Cleopas searched the stranger's face for hints of recognition or loyalties as they began walking. With the finesse of a drunkard, Isaac spewed his convictions and confusion. "We had hoped he was the one to redeem Israel."

Cleopas cringed as they crossed the bridge at the bottom of the valley between Jerusalem and Emmaus— between what they had hoped for and what had happened. *We had hoped.* What were they to do now? Walk around confessing their missteps, announcing they had fallen for a farce? Grief overtook his anger. Jesus had been their friend and teacher. He was not a deceiver! Was he? Below them, the brook chattered and pulled reeds into its current, straining to pluck them from the banks and drag them out to sea.

As they stepped from the bridge and began to climb the hill toward Emmaus, Cleopas thought Isaac would rein in his loose tongue, but Isaac prattled on about the women, the angels, and the vision and finally concluded by saying, "But the men never saw Jesus."

It was true. Peter and John had returned to the

house that morning panting and bewildered. Like a fool, Peter had run straight into the tomb and reported the impossible: burial wrappings collapsed in on themselves and a folded linen shroud lying beside them. It was the last push Cleopas had needed to escape the city.

"How foolish you are!" the stranger chided.

There it was again, a reminder of his folly.

"Are you so slow to believe all that the prophets wrote in the Scriptures?" he continued. "Wasn't it clearly predicted that the Messiah would have to suffer all these things before entering his glory?"*

Suffer? The Messiah would be victorious. Israel would be powerful under his rule. *A king like that wouldn't be nailed on a cross by the will of his own people.* Cleopas shook his head, unable to explain a conundrum he couldn't untangle.

"Haven't you heard what Moses spoke?" the stranger asked. "At the very start he predicted that the Messiah would be wounded in the war against sin and evil."

Cleopas had never considered that Israel's triumphant victor might be wounded in the fight, but he remembered how God spoke to the serpent in the

---

* Luke 24:26 (NLT)

garden: "He will crush your head, and you will strike his heel."* Loose gravel crunched against the paving stones underfoot as Cleopas pondered.

The man went on. "When you recall the deliverance of God's people from Egypt, don't you know the perfect lamb had to be killed before its blood could be used as a sign of protection?"

A scene as familiar as his upbringing burst into color. Deliverance from Egypt was the foundation of every monument of faith and tradition they celebrated. The blood of a lamb provided deliverance from death. He recalled John the Baptist hollering from the river, "Behold the Lamb of God," and his heart thumped into his throat.

"And didn't the Holy Spirit speak through the mouth of David that the Messiah would be insulted and forsaken?"†

The painful prayer of Jesus ripped through Cleopas' heart. Sagging from a Roman cross, Jesus had sputtered the words of King David, calling for his Father. The stranger detailed scenes the prophet Isaiah had

---

* Genesis 3:15
† See Psalm 22.

written, and the images flashed upon Cleopas' heart. *A servant who sorrowed and suffered as he was pierced?**

Like flares on the horizon by which a soldier might orient himself in darkness, Scripture illuminated misunderstanding. Cleopas listened as their companion explained the writings of Moses, the prophets, and the psalmists as if everything written in them foretold the mission of the Messiah. Warm familiarity burned inside him, comforting and unexpected.

"He will come in his glory, a kind of glory you've never imagined," the stranger assured, "but only after his suffering."

Cleopas stole a glance at Isaac. His eyes were fixed on the road, his brow wrinkled in deep thought. How long had they been listening to this man's interpretation of the Scripture? Red rays shot skyward as the sun set before them. Nestled in the hillside shrubbery, like chicks in a nest, the few houses of Emmaus welcomed them.

Suffering and glory? The unlikely companions sparred inside his mind as Cleopas veered from the road toward home.

"It was good to travel with you," the man said.

---

* See Isaiah 53:3–5.

Cleopas stopped. The stranger raised his hand and waved, "Peace be with you."

"You're not going farther tonight, are you?" Cleopas asked. "Please…it's nearly evening. It wouldn't be safe to continue alone. Why don't you stay with us?" Cleopas' heart burned for more. Familiarity flickered, brightening the mystery, but he could not see it clearly.

"Yes!" insisted Isaac. "The day is almost over, and we haven't eaten since yesterday. Aren't you hungry?"

The stranger hesitated and squinted into the distance at the road ahead.

"My mother always has plenty on hand," Isaac assured.

"Surely you know the dangers that lie on the roadsides. Between soldiers, bandits, and wolves you're likely to…." Cleopas stopped. "We'd be glad to have you," he finished.

"I would be honored," said the stranger.

———

As expected, Isaac's mother had spread the table with fruit and cheese, olive oil and butter. The familiar smells of roasted lamb and baked bread warmed the room, and Cleopas peeked into the kitchen. He was famished.

Isaac's family welcomed the fellow traveler. His presence blunted Isaac's father's scorn as they visited and reclined around the table. Isaac's mother poured milk and wine and set a warm loaf in front of Isaac's father as he spoke. "Your friend is well educated in the Scripture."

Isaac nodded. His father pushed the plate of bread toward their guest. "Will you bless our meal?"

He smiled, lifted the bread from the plate, turned his face heavenward, and began to thank God. He prayed as though conversing with a friend or a father. The prayer was familiar, but different. With the "Amen," he tore the loaf. Crumbs scattered on the table like manna sprinkled on the desert floor. Reaching across the table, he served steaming pieces to Isaac and Cleopas.

Cleopas slid the bread from his hand as if pulling a drawer. He froze. In their guest's palm, tender skin, freshly scarred, formed an almond shape, as if it had been pierced.

Cleopas gasped. Isaac leaned forward. They stole a glance at one another, groping for words. The kitchen fire snapped. Isaac's father gulped wine. A loaf of bread thumped as it dropped and rattled a plate.

He was gone.

Cleopas scrambled to his feet. The table jostled as Isaac pushed himself away. His mother stood in the doorway holding a plate of meat at an angle, broth running onto the floor. A goblet rolled in circles on the floor as Isaac's father stammered questions he couldn't finish.

"It was him," Isaac whispered.

The flicker that had warmed his heart earlier as they traveled now burst into white brilliance in Cleopas' mind. Light sorted confusion into comprehension. "Wasn't your heart burning as he explained the Scripture to us on the road!" Cleopas panted though he'd only voiced a single thought.

Isaac nodded in agreement and quoted Isaiah. "'It was the Lord's will to crush him and cause him to suffer, and though the Lord makes his life an offering for sin, he will see his offspring and prolong his days, and the will of the Lord will prosper in his hand. After he has suffered, he will see the light of life and be satisfied.'"*

---

* Isaiah 53:10–11

"We've got to go back to Jerusalem!"

Good news of their resurrected Savior revived more radiant hope than they had ever dared imagine. They rushed into the night, brash and bold, batting the truth back and forth. "It is true. He is risen."

Shocking Ignorance

Excitement and wonder are restless, and good news makes frightened disciples bold. From our angle it sheds a humorous light on their afternoon conversation.

Cleopas' questions for the unidentified stranger swim with irony. "Are you the only one visiting Jerusalem who does not know the things that have happened there in these days?"* Here was Jerusalem's eternal ruler, who wept for the citizens knowing they would reject his rescue. No, he was not a visitor. He was the rightful king temporarily deposed. But Cleopas didn't know it at the time. We can imagine him raising a skeptical eyebrow as this lone individual showed he had not paid the least bit of attention to current events.

---

* Luke 24:18

His question strikes us as almost irritated, like a widow leaving a funeral home, forced to answer a blundering stranger's "How's it going?"

It seems that Cleopas wondered how on earth the stranger could have been in Jerusalem and missed it all. In the parlance of modern English, we might roll our eyes and demand, "Have you been living under a rock?"

Of course, Jesus knew. He permitted betrayal. Blood seeped from his forehead as he sweat in the garden. Flesh tore from his back at the hands of a Roman scourging. Nails pierced his hands. He suffocated on the cross in place of those who killed him. Hidden in the cleft of a rock—or a tomb—God raised him. Indeed, he had been living under a rock, but only for a moment.

Of the three travelers on that road that day, Jesus was the only one who knew without a doubt.

Because Jesus was patient and desired to heighten their astonishment, he allowed them to detail what he already knew. Angels wore lightning. Guards sprawled outside the tomb. Women couldn't find a dead man in a tomb. Face to face with the One they grieved, the two men could not believe such absurdity.

From our angle, their disbelief is more laughable than

the resurrection, because we know what they didn't. It was Jesus himself who "came up and walked along with them."*

Mysteries Hidden in Plain Sight

In the valley between Jerusalem and Emmaus, in the confusion of an engrossing dispute, "they were kept from recognizing him."† Luke does not write that "they were too dull to recognize Jesus." Neither does he chide them for their slowness—he leaves that to Jesus. Luke says they were *prevented* from seeing clearly. Someone planned that these two disciples, who had walked with, listened to, and eaten with Jesus before his death, should not recognize him in his resurrected body.

God's wise and powerful hands had supernaturally covered their eyes. But it wasn't the harsh cruelty of a criminal blinding his hostage. They were not God's victims. They were his beloved children.

In the same way, a father might cover his daughter's eyes before her birthday party where guests are

---

* Luke 24:15
† Luke 24:16

smiling and silent, waiting for him to give the long-awaited signal to shout "Surprise!" When her eyes are uncovered, she does not hate him for keeping it a secret. All the balloons, cake, family and friends, games, and gifts were prepared to be revealed when her father knew she would experience the greatest joy.

She remembers a bakery receipt on the counter, a brown package on the doorstep, and her grandmother on the phone saying, "See you soon." Mysteries hidden in plain sight come tumbling together to astound. Her father's loving plans are finally unveiled, and the memory of details she did not understand enhances her thrill!

The Emmaus disciples were unknowingly held in the embrace of a Father who did the same for them. When they rushed back to Jerusalem to tell Peter and John and the others, you can hear them laughing and reciting Scriptures that make perfect sense considering Christ's resurrection.

God covered their eyes, so to speak, as he led them down the road to the surprise of their lives. He raised their hope by resurrecting their Savior. He "made his light shine in their hearts to give them the knowledge of God's glory displayed in the face of Christ."* They

---

* 2 Corinthians 4:6

had hoped Jesus was the one to redeem Israel, and he was.

But God had more glory to unveil. Within seven weeks of their supper with a stranger, in an upper room of Jerusalem, God would reveal another flaming gift. Jesus would not merely live to walk beside them on the road or sit before them at the table. He would go away to his Father so His Spirit could live *in* them.*

A Mystery for You and Me

Throughout the New Testament the apostle Paul writes about "the mystery that has been kept hidden for ages."† We can't quite wrap our heads around it as we walk through the valley between earthly suffering and eternal glory. But Paul explained it this way: "Christ in you, the hope of glory."‡

We too are on a road, not to Emmaus but to our eternal home in heaven, and it's easy to become discouraged. From our vantage point, suffering rarely

---

* See John 16:7.
† Colossians 1:26
‡ Colossians 1:27

makes sense, and a sinless eternity is light-years away. We have read of the promises of victory through Christ, of being made like him, of his glorious inheritance kept for us in heaven, but misunderstanding and incomplete information stir up confusion and questions.

Jesus sends his Spirit into our confusion—even if we don't recognize him at first—to remind and teach us what he's promised in his word.* What we view as an improbable wish he has guaranteed as an absolute reality. We long for visons of glory and glimpses of what heaven might be like while all along Christ, the hope of glory, resides inside believers, guaranteeing the riches of his inheritance.

Like the delighted daughter and the Emmaus disciples, we too will have the joy of looking back at our confusion with the relief of perfect comprehension. We will have the pleasure of connecting the dots between Scriptures read, sermons heard, and questions whispered among believing friends. With our faith made sight, the brilliant fullness of the good news of Jesus Christ will burst into radiant clarity, and we will see the glory of God in the face of Christ.

---

* See John 14:26.

With such certainty living in us, we are compelled to rush boldly to share the good news with our friends and family who may not yet know.

~

Dear Lord,

I wallow in the valley between what was once clear and what has turned out to be confusing. You spoke through your word and your spirit and I believed, but my experiences confuse. I confess I have doubted your words, your goodness, and your timing. You said that if I love and obey you, you'd show yourself to me. I do love you, Lord, but sometimes I struggle to see you.

You promised your Spirit to instruct and teach me in the way I should go. Still, I find myself stalled at unmarked intersections, peering into the distance, holding a finger in the wind, listening for direction.

You promised to be with me always, to the end of the age, but I grope at the air, searching for your presence.

Open my eyes to see you manifested in the sights I encounter—on the road, at the table, in a stranger.

Give me ears to hear your guidance from your written word—words you recorded in millennia past that still provide meaning and perspective. Give me wisdom to discern between your generous prompting and what I fear might be my own conjured ideas.

Help me recognize your presence as you connect the dots you've carefully arranged. Engrave your truth in my mind to remind me that though your timing may be inexplicable and your hand unrecognizable, you will eventually make perfect, holy sense of it all.

Thank you for delighting me with glorious mystery you spotlight at the perfect moment. What a privilege. What a Savior.

Conclusion

The Disappointment That Made Hope Possible

At the heart of these stories of God's "strength for today and bright hope for tomorrow"[15] lies a divine irony. Our hope was born of Jesus' disappointment.

Perhaps it's inaccurate to speak of Jesus being disappointed. It indicates an element of surprise, and since he is God, he can't be surprised. But when we see him suffering in the Garden of Gethsemane, the word *disappointment* is a diluted description. The Gospel writers say he was anguished.*

"My soul is overwhelmed with sorrow to the point of death," Jesus said.†

"Everything is possible for you," he prayed.‡ "Father, if you are willing, take this cup from me; yet not my

---

* Luke 22:44
† Mark 14:34
‡ Mark 14:36

will, but yours be done."* Jesus knew what he must do, but he asked his Father about it anyway.

After he prayed, "an angel from heaven appeared to him and strengthened him. And being in anguish, he prayed more earnestly, and his sweat was like drops of blood falling to the ground."†

These are the painful words and experiences of the perfect Son of God pleading with his Father as he approached his ultimate act of obedience. The writer of Hebrews tells us Jesus was "tempted in every way, just as we are—yet he did not sin."‡ In the garden, as he cried to his Father about the unimaginable horror of crucifixion and abandonment, Jesus remained sinless.

God did not answer him audibly, but we know his response because we've read the rest of the story: "It is possible, but I am not willing." God could have sent thousands upon thousands of angels to rescue Jesus from his suffering. It wouldn't have required a *single* angel. God could have spoken, and Jesus would have been spared. But he didn't say a word.

The gavel fell, and Jesus was sentenced. "You must

* Luke 22:42
† Luke 22:43–44
‡ Hebrews 4:15

drink this cup. You must suffer the full extent of my wrath over sin. You must endure being forsaken and the fury of my justice so that our beloved creation will not have to." God was not willing to abort the plan because he loved us, and he loved Jesus.

As Jesus sweat anguished drops of blood, God sent an angel not to deliver Jesus from suffering but to strengthen and revive him to finish the work. Jesus received glory and we received hope.

Forged from "Disappointment"

What is this hope? We can know, without a doubt, that Jesus Christ initiated a scandalous and merciful exchange when he died. On the cross, Jesus accepted the punishment we deserved for our sin committed against him. He suffered the consequences for all the ways we've wronged God—past, present, and future. But he didn't leave us with a blank slate, erased of all our sin.

He also gave us his righteous record. That clean slate has been marked up again, but not with a record of our wrongdoing. It has been filled with the righteous record of Jesus. Everything he did perfectly has been applied to you and written on your slate!* Martin Luther called it "the Great Exchange."

Our salvation has past, present, and future implications. In the *past*, at the cross, Jesus died for the sins of the whole world. Because God raised Jesus from the dead, he has *presently* given us his Holy Spirit, through whom God makes us more like Jesus. In the *future*, we will be ushered into an inheritance bought and prepared for us by Jesus.

Hope for This Life

The assurance of a glorious future reality does not automatically alleviate ongoing pain in this life. In a dying marriage, the glory of heaven doesn't numb the sadness. To the parent sitting in the waiting room of pediatric oncology, that bright future is barely visible. To the Christian battered by a series of small disasters, eternity with Jesus is a long way off, and the way forward is strewn with more trouble.

Jesus was familiar with long-term sadness. The prophet Isaiah writes of Jesus, "He was a man of

---

* See 2 Corinthians 5:21.

sorrows, acquainted with deepest grief."* At the pinnacle of his obedience, Jesus was engulfed in agony, and his Father sent an angel to strengthen him.

In despair and distress, God will supply all we need to hold fast to him. We've observed it repeatedly.

Simeon heard a promise. "You will see the Lord's Christ."†

John the Baptist clung to secondhand encouragement. "You will be blessed if you don't fall away on account of the way I operate."‡

The demoniac of Gadara was commissioned. "Return home and tell what the Lord has done for you."§

Martha received a next-step instruction. "Believe, and you will see the glory of God."¶

Jairus took courage. "Don't be afraid; just believe."**

Peter jumped at the chance to relieve his fright, fatigue, and longing. "It is I. Come."††

Mary was reminded of her all-powerful God and

---

* Isaiah 53:3
† See Luke 2:26.
‡ See John 7:23.
§ See Mark 5:19.
¶ See John 11:40.
** Mark 5:36
†† See Matthew 14:27–29.

his provision. "Dear woman, here is a son who will care for you after I'm gone."*

The Emmaus disciples gained a crystal-clear explanation of how all Scripture pointed to Jesus as Jesus, "explained to them what was said in all the Scriptures concerning himself"†

God revived their hope in ways they never could have imagined. Each word of warning, confirmation, and instruction was a means to solidify their hope of his promised future. He will do the same for us. Our hope is a confident expectation—"an anchor for the soul, firm and secure."‡

A Cord of Three Strands

Shipmen can observe tension in the rope that fastens the anchor to the vessel. It alternately tightens and becomes slack as the ship rises and falls with the waves, and they know they're not drifting off course. Likewise, believers in Jesus observe the braided

---

* See John 19:26–27.
† Luke 24:27
‡ Hebrews 6:19

strands of God's word, his Spirit, and prayer as evidence that we are held fast.

In God's word we read of his past faithfulness. Our faith is strengthened, and our assurance grows. The apostle Paul writes, "Everything that was written in the past was written to teach us, so that through the endurance taught in the Scriptures and the encouragement they provide we might have hope."*

The work of the Holy Spirit, who convicts, teaches, and comforts believers, is proof of our attachment to hope. Paul tells us, "The promised Holy Spirit is a deposit guaranteeing our inheritance until the redemption of those who are God's possession—to the praise of his glory."† Our hope is secured because God's Spirit lives in us.

As we speak and listen to God in prayer, he fosters affection and confidence that he can change circumstances or hearts—whichever he deems best. Whether we pray daily for decades or cry for help as we sink, we expose our dependence on Jesus and become "joyful in hope, patient in affliction, faithful in prayer."‡

---

* Romans 15:4
† Ephesians 1:14
‡ Romans 12:12

These tightly twisted cords are the fibers of faith, and "faith is the assurance of things hoped for, the conviction of things not seen."* God's firm reliability is the reason we can be sure of what we cannot see. It is not based on performance, understanding, or feelings. The steadfast certainty of our hope relies on God's unwavering faithfulness.

Unseen Certainty

The anchored ship is an apt picture of the hope God gives us through Jesus. He has gone before us, Hebrews says, into God's presence behind "the curtain," where we cannot see him with our eyes. Likewise, when the anchor is lodged in the seafloor it's hidden from sight. Waves crash over the boat's railing and the hull creaks under the strain, but shipmen expect the unseen to hold firm.

"In this world you will have trouble," Jesus said. The stories we've examined are proof. Simeon waited decades. John's ministry was extreme and brief. The demoniac of Gadara had scars as a testimony to his

---

* Hebrews 11:1 (ESV)

rescue. Jairus, Mary, and Martha witnessed the agonizing decline of loved ones. Peter must have been spiritually dizzy from swinging between devotion and doubt. As Mary witnessed the murder of her blameless son, her soul was pierced. And when hope was dashed on the rocks of Golgotha, the Emmaus disciples walked away from everything they'd anticipated. God's people are not spared the battering waves of uncertainty and trouble.

But for those who've placed their hope in Christ, discouragement and confusion are not indicators that the mooring has come loose. Regardless of how we feel or how well we understand our circumstances, we are bound to a fixed hope.

"Fasten the little vessel of your life to that great anchor, Christ, who has died, and who lives for you. And then, though the thread between you and Him be but slender and fragile, it will not be a dead cable, but a living nerve, along which His own steadfast life will pour, making you steadfast like Himself, and at last fulfilling and transcending your highest hopes in eternal fruition of His own blessedness."[16]

Christ Jesus is our remarkable hope, and he does not disappoint.

Acknowledgments

Metaphors for collaborative efforts abound—a team, a symphony, a village, and of course, the body of Christ. Each whole group consists of many individual parts in desperate need of the others. Though writing may seem like a solitary effort, I am exceedingly thankful for what so many have contributed. There would not be a book without you.

Many thanks to...

Dan Balow, for your level-headed and witty advice and direction.

Adrienne Ingrum and the FaithWords team, for the opportunity to write and publish. Thank you for taking a chance on me.

Yolanda, for being a voracious reader, insightful thinker, and encourager extraordinaire. Thank you for sharing your story, your gifts, and your wealth of knowledge with me. Your prayer for this book means so much. You are a treasure!

My book prayer team, for lifting up my "nonurgent" prayer requests. Book writing doesn't fall in the same category as family health or tragedy, but your intercession is the reason you're holding this book. Thank you for being my sisters in Christ.

The Hope*Writers community, which is easily the happiest and most encouraging place on the internet. Thank you for freely sharing your experiences and suggestions.

Readers who have written, emailed, commented on social media, and shared these stories with friends. Your encouragement has fueled my desire to keep pointing to the magnificence of Jesus. Thank you for blessing me.

Friends and family who have celebrated the small and large milestones with me along the way with cheesecake or lunch, by email or emoji.

My boys, for folding laundry every week so I could devote more time to writing and for the fist bumps upon manuscript completion.

Kurt, for keeping yourself awake on all the road trips where I read and studied in silence as you drove, for being my best marketer, and for supporting me in what sounded like a pipe dream. I love you.

Jesus Christ, who accepts the meager offering of words as worship even though they fall short of the perfection he deserves.

My warmest gratitude to you all.

Notes

Steadfast Hope

1. John Koessler, *The Surprising Grace of Disappointment: Finding Hope When God Seems to Fail Us* (Chicago: Moody Publishers, 2013), 48.

Questioning Hope

2. Flavius Josephus, *The Antiquities of the Jews*, in *Josephus: The Complete Works*, trans. William Whiston (Nashville, TN: Thomas Nelson, 1998), 581.
3. Darrell L. Bock, *Luke 1:1–9:50*, Baker Exegetical Commentary on the New Testament (Grand Rapids, MI: Baker Books, 1994), 581.

Redirected Hope

4. Alexander MacLaren, "Mark 5," *Expositions of Holy Scripture*, BibleHub, accessed 2/5/2018, http://biblehub.com/commentaries/maclaren/mark/5.htm.
5. MacLaren, "Mark 5."
6. Ken Gire, *Windows of the Soul: Hearing God in the Everyday Moments of Your Life* (Grand Rapids, MI: Zondervan, 1996), 71.

Despairing Hope

7. Koessler, *The Surprising Grace of Disappointment*.
8. Darlene Deibler Rose, *Evidence Not Seen: A Woman's Miraculous Faith in the Jungles of World War II* (New York: HarperCollins Publishers, 1988), 148.

9. Rose, *Evidence Not Seen*, 150.
10. Rose, *Evidence Not Seen*, 157.

Delayed Hope

11. Elisha A. Hoffman, "I Must Tell Jesus," 1894.
12. Alexander MacLaren, "John 11," *Expositions of Holy Scripture*, BibleHub, accessed 10/13/2017, http://biblehub.com/commentaries/maclaren/john/11.htm.
13. MacLaren, "John 11."

Confused Hope

14. The second person on the Emmaus road is not named in Scripture. I chose to call him Isaac for clarity's sake in retelling the story.

Conclusion

15. Lyric by Thomas Chisholm from "Great Is Thy Faithfulness," 1923.
16. Alexander MacLaren, "Hebrews 6," *Expositions of the Holy Scriptures*, BibleHub, accessed 9/19/2017, http://biblehub.com/commentaries/maclaren/hebrews/6.htm.

About the Author

Shauna Letellier is the author of *Remarkable Faith: When Jesus Marveled at Faith in Unremarkable People*. Her writing has been featured at Girlfriends in God, in the *Huffington Post*, Day Spring's (in)courage, the MOB Society, For Every Mom, and *MomSense* magazine (now called *Hello, Dearest*), a publication of MOPS International. She attended Focus on the Family's Focus Leadership Institute and is a graduate of Grace University in Omaha, Nebraska. With degrees in family and biblical studies, she teaches in her local church and writes regularly at shaunaletellier.com. Shauna lives in South Dakota with her husband and three sons.

Also by Shauna Letellier

*Remarkable Faith: When Jesus Marveled
at the Faith of Unremarkable People*